HOW TO DESTROY WESTERN CIVILIZATION AND OTHER IDEAS FROM THE CULTURAL ABYSS

T0060612

PETER J. KREEFT

How to Destroy Western Civilization and Other Ideas from the Cultural Abyss

IGNATIUS PRESS   SAN FRANCISCO

Cover art: jrwasserman, iStockphoto.com

Cover design by Riz Boncan Marsella

© 2021 by Ignatius Press, San Francisco
All rights reserved
ISBN 978-1-62164-268-8 (PB)
ISBN 978-1-64229-159-9 (eBook)
Library of Congress Control Number 2020946601
Printed in the United States of America ∞

Contents

How to Destroy Western Civilization

The single most necessary thing we can possibly do to save our civilization—the single most necessary thing citizens can *ever* do to save their civilization, at all times and all places and in all cultures, whether they are good or evil, religious or irreligious, ancient or modern—is to have children.

If you don't have children, your civilization will cease to exist. Before you can be good or evil, religious or irreligious, you must exist.

Having children is thus the most rational thing we can do. It is also the most trans-rational thing we can do. I remember hearing someone say once that "Having fits is more rational than having children." They were quite right! But the conclusion they thought followed from that ("So don't have children") did not follow. Having fits is more rational than falling in love, too. And having fits is more rational than being a saint (which is falling in love with God), being a martyr, or even being a hero.

Having children is the most heroic thing we can do because nothing changes your life more than having children. Martyrdom is easy; it's over quickly. Children are never over. Never. Not even if they die before you.

Children are the masters; parents are the servants. The parents' life, their time, their lifetime, their money, their attention, *everything*, changes and orbits like a planet around the sun of their children's needs. Having children is the single most generous, charitable, loving, unselfish, saintly Christian act that a society can perform for itself.

It is the act of self-giving, and the first thing that parents give is the first thing the parents have: existence. It is very obvious, but easily forgotten, that no subsequent gifts —love, education, support, attention—can be given if that first gift (existence) is denied, or if that gift is taken away after it is given, by murdering the children that already exist. (One-third of all children conceived in America and Canada are aborted; I think our ancestors would literally not be able to believe that fact.)

Today you hear many people in our civilization—the one that used to be called "Christendom" and is now called simply "modern Western civilization" and whose most accurate name theologically is "apostate Christendom"—give an astonishing explanation, or reason, to justify not having children or killing the children they already have. You hear this especially from men, who cannot feel the child inside the womb and who can "relate to" the child as a real entity only after (and if) he is born. The explanation is that "I wouldn't want to bring children into a world like this. It's an irresponsible act to bring children into this world."

What do they mean by that? They can mean only two possible things: that the world is bad for children either materially or spiritually.

The primary concerns of people who say this are almost always not spiritual but material. When you ask them what's wrong with the world, they never say there is not enough religion. They say there is not enough peace, prosperity, security, comfort, health care, or environmental responsibility. In other words, not enough human control over nature and human nature. They do not think that the new Baconian "*summum bonum*" of "Man's conquest of Nature" is overdone; they think it is underdone.

To see how blatantly hypocritical this reasoning is—in other words, to see that those who say this are literally lying, at least to themselves—just look at the facts. Of all the civilizations in the history of the world, our modern Western civilization—Europe and North America—is the very *best* civilization ever into which to bring children by those very materialistic standards that the people who give this excuse are using.

No civilization ever had as much money as we do. Even the moderately poor today have more stuff, and more money to buy stuff, than the moderately rich of any past civilizations.

No civilization ever had as much knowledge and power, that is, science and technology, as we have. The Baconian project has worked spectacularly well. The average person before the twentieth century experienced at least ten times as much pain, perhaps 100 times as much pain, in his life as the average person today. Health, comfort, cures, and lifespan, brought about by medical technology, are spectacularly better than ever before. That fact is not controversial, nor is its desirability.

There is still much war and violence in the world, but not nearly as much of it here in America as there is in most of the rest of the world. Americans and Europeans hesitate to visit the Middle East or Latin America or even China because of the violence and danger and repression there, but citizens of these countries do not hesitate to visit America for that reason. Millions of refugees seek to immigrate to Europe or America; almost no one wants to emigrate out of Europe or America. Not one politician in Mexico, Palestine, Syria, or China is arguing for border fences to stop the immigrants from entering.

America suffered great and terrible losses in six wars: the Revolutionary War, the Civil War, two World Wars, the

Korean War, and the Vietnam War. Since then, the casualty rate has been far, far less.

America also suffered a Great Depression and a great crime wave during the Great Depression. Our recent recession was mild and short, and our current crime wave, by the standards of the past, is mild and getting milder.

That is the horrible world into which people refuse to bring their children.

It looks like nothing short of *Brave New World* will do for them, where the control is total and the pain is nonexistent.

But in *Brave New World*, children are manufactured, and there are no parents or families.

So that is the logic of the secularists, the children of the "Enlightenment", the people who think the world is too religious. What about the religious people? What is their take on our world?

They also judge the world as bad, but for the opposite reason: there is not enough religion; there is too much materialism. They say that the modern world is not better than the medieval world, but worse, even though it is materially richer, because it is spiritually poorer because it has lost God. They say that He counts more than refrigerators, contraceptives, airplanes, anesthetics, and even Viagra.

And yet these are the people who never say they do not want to bring children into this terrible world. They say (and do) the exact opposite: they have children, they sacrifice themselves, they "lay down their lives", literally, in sexual intercourse, not just for pleasure (of course that's a given, a universal), but also for children, for others. They do not complain about there being too many "others"; they think there are not *enough* "others", so they create more of them.

And by all scientific data (ask your insurance company), these people—religious people and people who have children—are the happiest. Just to mention the two most obvious criteria of happiness: they live the longest, and they commit suicide the least.

So who are the "enlightened" ones? Who are the ones who are standing in the light, who are telling the truth about their society and about themselves?

And who will survive, and who will not? Who can sing "The future belongs to us"?

So I wish we would stop playing Cassandra and start fighting our "culture war" with joy and confidence. For we wield the one weapon that will infallibly win the future: children.

2

What Can Chicken Little Do?

What can you do when you see the sky falling, when you see your culture swirling like garbage down the drain?

If you are Augustine, you can write *The City of God*, the world's first, greatest, and most Christian philosophy of history. If you're not Augustine, but you know a little philosophy, you can still modestly gather wisdom as data to preserve and remember, like the monks in the Dark Ages.

Here is some relevant data—not empirical data, but philosophical data—that can guide us. Here are forty foundational, fundamental facts of common sense. I have organized it philosophically in seven categories: epistemological, theological, metaphysical, anthropological, ethical, political, and historical.

Data are important, in fact, necessary; they are the premises for our conclusions. But what I have not done is the harder and more important thing: I have not drawn particular practical consequences from these premises. I don't tell you here *how* to save Western civilization, or even whether it is savable.

Point 1: I begin with epistemology. Epistemology is about knowing. The first thing we need to know is this: we need to know the difference between what we know and what we don't know. That was the first principle for both Socrates and Confucius.

Point 2: We cannot be skeptics. We know that we know

some things. To quote J. Budziszewski's unforgettable phrase, there are things we can't not know. That even includes the thing that is the most necessary for a civilization to know and the thing our civilization is the first one in history to deny officially, the natural moral law.

(Besides, all forms of skepticism are self-contradictory: Do we know that we don't know? Is it certain that we're not certain? Is it objective truth that truth is not objective? Are there absolutely no absolutes?)

Point 3: We can't be dogmatic about ourselves, either. Much of what we think we know, we don't. That was one of the things Job learned. It was the same thing St. Catherine learned when God preached the shortest sermon in history to her, summarizing all of divine revelation in four words: "I'm God, you're not."

Point 4: We know that our most certain knowledge is divine revelation, since God alone can neither deceive nor be deceived.

Point 5: Our next most certain knowledge is experience, that is, our past, our history, both individual and collective.

Point 6: We know that the four most important questions we can ask about any practical problem are the four steps of a medical analysis: the observation of the symptoms, the diagnosis of the disease, the prognosis of the cure, and the prescription for the treatment. They correspond to Aristotle's four causes. The symptoms are the material cause, the disease is the formal cause, the prognosis is the final cause, and the prescription is the efficient cause. Buddha's "four noble truths" give his answers to these four questions: to live is to suffer (suffering is the symptom), the cause of suffering is desire (desire is the disease), the abolition of desire is the abolition of suffering (*nirvana*, or extinction, is the prognosis), and the way to the abolition of desire is the noble eightfold path of ego-reduction. Jesus' four noble truths are death, sin, eternal life, and faith in Christ, God's gift of grace. "The wages of sin is death, but the free gift of God is eternal life in Christ Jesus our Lord."

Apply these four steps to our cultural and moral decline, and what do you get? That might be a good way to begin our discussions.

For instance: the most obvious and radical symptom of our sudden decline, and the cause of many of the other symptoms, especially the decline of stable families, is the Sexual Revolution. What was the deeper disease that caused and motivated that revolution (and the more general revolution of moral relativism that was needed to justify it)? It was, as Solzhenitsyn so simply said in his 1983 Templeton Prize address, that "we have forgotten God." As Aquinas said (also very simply), when a man is deprived of true, spiritual joy, he must become addicted to carnal pleasures to fill the vacuum. Is there an optimistic prognosis? Yes. The cure is conversion, of mind, of will, of heart, and of life. And the only way to the conversion of a culture is the conversion of individuals, beginning with ourselves and every individual with whom we come in contact.

Next come some relevant truths we know from revealed theology.

Point 7: God exists, and God is God. God is the God of the Bible; God is the God of Jesus Christ. That is our non-negotiable absolute. If Muslims are more certain than we that there is no God but God, they will inherit the corpse of our civilization.

Point 8: God is sovereign. He's got the whole world in His hands. His providence is mysterious but real. History is His story. We, too, write the story, but only as characters in His story, not independent of it.

Point 9: God makes all things, even evils, work together

for good for those who love him—and this applies to cultures as well as to individuals. God blesses nations as well as individuals when they obey His will and His law and punishes them when they disobey. That includes all Ten Commandments, including both Thou Shalt Not Kill and Thou Shalt Not Commit Adultery. He's not satisfied with moral specializations, from either Christians or Muslims.

Point 10: Faith and love, prayer and adoration, what Muslims call "surrender", open doors to God's activity. "Let it be to me according to your word" brought Christ down. It was meant to continue. Christ is Jacob's Ladder. On Him Heaven's angels descend and earth's prayers ascend like commuter traffic on a global highway. Prayer is power. If every Catholic in America practiced Eucharistic adoration fifteen minutes every day, we would see the greatest religious revival in human history.

Point 11: Mary is Satan's most feared enemy. She is the patroness of the Americas. What she did in Mexico City almost five hundred years ago she can do again, especially since the same demon that was worshipped by the Aztecs with the blood of children is being worshipped and obeyed in America.

Point 12: Spiritual warfare is real. Wars on earth always reflect wars in Heaven. Life is jihad, holy war. Too many Muslims think the enemy is flesh and blood, and too many Christians think there is no enemy at all. The devils laugh at us both.

Point 13: This world and this life are precious, but Man's ultimate good, end, purpose, and happiness are eternal, not temporal. Ephemeral civilizations are to immortal souls what fleas are to galaxies. Those who seek first the kingdom of this world lose not only the kingdom of God but this world as well. That is what C. S. Lewis sagely calls the principle of first and second things.

Now some relevant principles of metaphysics.

Point 14: Invisible reality dwarfs visible reality, which is like an epidermis or the surface of the ocean. That's even true of matter; how much more of spirit? Hamlet is right: there are more things in heaven and earth, not fewer things, than are dreamed of in our philosophy.

Point 15: Yet matter is not only real but holy. We are saved only by the body and the blood, by "This is My Body", not by "This is My mind."

Point 16: Spirit, not matter, is the source of power. As the wind moves the trees, spirit moves matter, design moves evolution, souls move bodies, and good or bad philosophies move good or bad civilizations. Wars are won by soul strength. That's why the nation that defeated Hitler lost to Ho Chi Minh.

We move to some points of anthropology.

Point 17: Man has free will. Therefore, repentance is always possible, even for societies. But repentance and conversion are easier for individuals than for societies.

Point 18: Man has free will. Therefore, ever-increasing evil is also possible, leading inevitably to self-destruction, both temporal and eternal, and both individual and collective.

Point 19: Man has free will. Therefore, neither of these two outcomes is necessary or predictable. That is why history is a drama, not a science.

Point 20: Every man is an end in himself. Man is the only creature God created for his own sake. Cultures, civilizations, nations, and even religions exist for man, not man for them. And they are judged by how well they serve man, not by how well man serves them. A good society is, as Dorothy Day says, simply a society that makes it easier for man to be good.

Point 21: Though man is fallen, he remembers Eden and

hungers for Heaven. He cannot help admiring saints. There is a spiritual gravity, which the Chinese call *Te*. Moral goodness is winsome. But it also provokes hate: saints often become martyrs. But the blood of the martyrs is the most powerful seed of the Church. When love and suffering meet, unstoppable power is released.

This brings us to related ethical principles.

Point 22: The natural moral law cannot be totally erased from the human heart.

Point 23: Yet the same St. Thomas who says that also says that many parts of the natural law can be erased temporarily from our consciousness by evil habits, especially sexual addictions, which are the most passionate and powerful and, therefore, the most blinding and deceptive.

Point 24: There is a continuity of issues in sexual morality. It's a one-piece camel, and once the camel's nose gets under the tent, the rest of the camel follows, including the stinky parts. Once sexual pleasure is divorced from procreation by contraception, anything goes, including the deliberate murder of one's own innocent unborn children (for abortion is only backup contraception, after all) and the sacrilegious exaltation of sodomy (one of the four "sins that cry to heaven") as a form of marriage (the first sacrament and an image of the Trinity itself).

Point 25 is the principle of first and second things. Goods are in a hierarchy, and whenever a greater good, or "first thing", is sacrificed to a lesser good, or "second thing", not only is the "first thing" lost (willingly) but the "second thing" is also lost (unwillingly). This is the psychology of addiction: it spoils the very pleasure it was designed to deliver.

Here is C. S. Lewis' application of this principle to our current problem:

Was civilisation ever seriously endangered until civilisation became the exclusive aim of human activity? There is much rash idealisation of past ages about, and I do not wish to encourage more of it. Our ancestors were cruel, lecherous, greedy and stupid, like ourselves. But while they cared for other things more than for civilisation . . . was civilisation often in serious danger of disappearing?

Point 26: A crucial example of our reversal of first and second things is the relation between truth and freedom. Freedom is for truth, not truth for freedom. Deny truth, and you destroy freedom. The truth makes you free; freedom does not make you true.

Now some points about politics.

Point 27: Politics is not absolute. Politics is not religion. In the People's Republic of Massachusetts, we are political about our religion and religious about our politics. That is our idolatry.

Point 28: Politics is human, honorable, and important. Man is a political animal.

Point 29: Nations need God just as much as individuals do. They even have guardian angels. Ours needs help.

Point 30: Though good nations can be pluralistically religious, they cannot be irreligious.

Point 31: A nation that does not know the meaning of life, that has no substantive philosophy, has no wisdom and no real authority to decide anything, for example, whether a city's budget should fund a new library or a new casino.

Point 32: If Jesus Christ came to earth today, He would not totally support either party's platform. He would either refuse to vote or He would hold His nose and vote for the Republicans because Democrats deny the precondition for all other rights, the right to life, to His own dear children. Mother Teresa said, "When a mother can kill her own child, what is left of the West to save?"

Point 33: Individuals should serve the common good, and the common good should serve individuals. One for all, and all for one. Both libertarian individualism and socialistic collectivism are perversions.

Point 34: Subsidiarity is crucial. Larger bodies interfering with jobs that smaller bodies can do is the road to totalitarianism. Our totalitarianism is not hard but soft; not *1984*, but *Brave New World*.

Finally, some points about the philosophy of history.

Point 35: All healthy cultures have had *pietas*, respect for gods and ancestors, that is, tradition. We disrespect not only our unborn children but also our dead parents.

Point 36: All healthy cultures have had a high regard for families. The four longest-lasting ones in history are the four most family-friendly ones: Jewish (3500 years), Confucian (2100 years), Islamic (1400 years), and Roman (700 years).

Point 37: All healthy cultures have believed in the natural moral law. Ours is the first whose mind-molders, both official and unofficial (media), do not. We are certainly doomed to extinction unless this is reversed, because there is simply no alternative. (Denial of any universal, objective, and absolute moral law also imperils one's salvation, for if there is no law, there is no sin, and if there is no sin, there is no repentance, and if there is no repentance, there is no salvation.)

Point 38: The enemy within is far worse than the enemy without. Islamic terrorists can only kill a few bodies; our own home-grown apostates and immoralists can kill our souls.

Point 39: Like us, our culture and its civilizational body are mortal. A thousand years from now, America will not exist. But you will. And so will Israel and the Catholic Church, on earth. God does not welsh on His covenants.

Point 40: A few saints can change the world. History is

made, not by those who try to make history, but by those who humbly but obstinately obey God's will no matter what and let the chips fall where they may. To echo Mother Teresa again, God put us in this world, not to be successful, but to be faithful.

What can you do to help save our civilization? I'm not sure. But I am sure that you can do something infinitely more important than helping to save our civilization. By your words and your works you can help save something infinitely more important than that. A single eternal soul is more valuable than the entire mortal universe.

I close with this essential Christian vision, from C.S. Lewis' golden sermon "The Weight of Glory":

> It is a serious thing to live in a society of possible gods and goddesses, to remember that the dullest and most uninteresting person you can talk to may one day be a creature which, if you saw it now, you would be strongly tempted to worship, or else a horror and a corruption such as you now meet, if at all, only in a nightmare. All day long we are, in some degree, helping each other to one or other of these destinations. It is in the light of these overwhelming possibilities, it is with the awe and circumspection proper to them, that we should conduct all our dealings with one another, all friendships, all loves, all play, all politics. There are no *ordinary* people. You have never met a mere mortal. Nations, cultures, arts, civilisations—these are mortal, and their life is to ours as the life of a gnat. But it is immortals whom we joke with, work with, marry, snub, and exploit —immortal horrors or everlasting splendours.

3

The Unmentionable Elephant
in the Living Room of the
Religious Liberty Debate

We are seeing a number of historic firsts in the infancy of the new millennium.

First, the flagship Catholic university, named after the most pro-life Woman in history, rewarded the most pro-abortion president in history by giving him an honorary degree. On this occasion, the president publicly promised to respect Catholic conscience rights by keeping a conscience clause exception in his comprehensive health-care program.

He lied. He reneged on his promise.

The result was a second first: for the first time in recent American history, every single Catholic bishop stood up and drew a line in the sand and said "Not possible!" on a controversial and unpopular issue.

The administration's "compromise" was that the new law forcing Catholics to pay for abortifacient contraception would not be implemented for a year. Cardinal Dolan of New York said, "They have given us twelve months to figure out how to compromise our consciences."

Why has the Obama administration, for the first time in American history, deliberately trampled on the two most absolute and nonnegotiable rights and liberties of humanity, moral (conscience) and religious? Such a large and momentous effect must have a sufficiently large and momentous cause.

It's the unmentionable elephant in the living room. It's sex. Religious liberty is being attacked in the name of sexual liberty.

The current culture war is most fundamentally about abortion, and abortion is about sex. Abortion is backup contraception, and contraception is the demand to have sex without having babies. If storks brought babies, Planned Parenthood would go broke.

Catholics, Muslims, Orthodox Jews, and Evangelical Protestants are the only groups left in the West who oppose the Sexual Revolution and uphold traditional sexual morality. Everyone else assumes, without question or controversy, that contraception has finally "liberated" sex from its servile connection with baby-making and has turned it into a purely personal, "recreational" option.

Our liberty is being denied because it threatens their liberty. Religious liberty threatens sexual liberty. Our religious freedom of conscience threatens their sexual freedom of conscience.

It's not their behavior that we threaten, it's their conscience. They want us to approve their behavior, at least implicitly, by paying for it. We are the last people in our culture who say no, who judge, who dare to play the prophet. Prophets are always unpopular. There's no profit in being a prophet. Prophets are lights that are a bit too bright. They show up the artificiality in the air-brushed *Playboy* fantasies. They threaten the fun. Prophets are X-rays that show cancers to patients who are living in denial.

If Jews and Christians could just erase two of the Commandments, the ones against adultery and lust, the new post-Christian culture of Western civilization would have absolutely no problem with religion.

They call us "judgmental" and "authoritarian", but it's

because we are exactly the opposite, because we do *not* claim
the authority to contradict our Creator and Commander,
because we do not dare to be so judgmental as to judge
His judgments to be mistaken, because we dare not erase
or change the line He has drawn in the sand. We cannot
compromise our consciences because we believe our consciences are His prophets, not society's.

It's not that we seek to impose our sexual morality (or
any other part of morality) on others by force. We propose;
we do not impose. We seek only liberty of conscience for
everyone, including ourselves. No one wants to send sexual
storm troopers into fornicators' bedrooms.

But they seek to impose their sexual morality on us. They
do not merely propose, they impose. They want to force
us to compromise our consciences or be punished by a fine
(or something worse). Why? We can tolerate them; why
can't they tolerate us? Why are they so threatened by our
minority view?

Because they know it is not a minority view, but the
majority view in all times and places outside twenty-first-
century Europe and North America (for example, every culture in history and "backward" cultures like Africa and Latin
America still today) and the view of all the great religions
of the world. If our principles were merely quirky, like the
principles of a small Native American tribe that sees the hal-
lucinogenic peyote as a religious sacrament or the principles
of the Amish that see electricity as evil, the Establishment
would not be threatened by these principles and would read-
ily grant these fringe groups the right to be exceptional for
the sake of conscience—as they do. They do not insist that
the Amish pay a penalty for not using electricity. But they
do insist that we pay a penalty for not paying for abortions.

Why? Perhaps their consciences are still alive, after all, and feel guilty about killing their own unborn children. How could they not? If they can get us to compromise our consciences, they won't feel so bad about having compromised their own. "Everybody does it" has always been a very effective and convenient excuse for any kind of evil, even slavery or genocide.

That's why this is not just about contraception or abortion or whether every human biological life is intrinsically valuable. It's about whether every human conscience is. The Obama administration has said, in effect, that consciences are still to be respected (for example, pacifists will not be forced to fight in wars) *as long as they do not conflict with the Sexual Revolution.*

So we are at war. The two sides in the war are sexual "liberty" vs. religious liberty, which includes liberty of conscience.

Paradoxically, we are fighting for their consciences as well as our own. And they are fighting against their own consciences as well as ours.

Religious liberty will win. The defenders of religious liberty will win because we will never give up. We will never give up because we *can* never give up. But the other side can. We cannot tell God and our conscience that Caesar is our God. But they can do that. In fact, they have already done that once, and, therefore, they can do it again. They will eventually back down, and we never will. Never. They don't believe in a "never", in an eternity, in eternal principles, in absolutes. We do. It's as simple as that.

4

The Paradox of Poverty

The paradox I have in mind is stated best by C. S. Lewis, in *The Problem of Pain*, when speaking about the criticism from Marxists and other left-leaning secularists against Christianity's stance on suffering in general and poverty in particular:

> Those who reject Christianity will not be moved by Christ's statement that poverty is blessed. But here a rather remarkable fact comes to my aid. Those who would most scornfully repudiate Christianity as a mere "opiate of the people" have a contempt for the rich, that is, for all mankind *except* the poor. They regard the poor as the only people worth preserving from "liquidation", and place in them the only hope of the human race. But this is not compatible with a belief that the effects of poverty on those who suffer it are wholly evil; it even implies that they are good. The Marxist thus finds himself in real agreement with the Christian in those two beliefs which Christianity paradoxically demands—that poverty is blessed and yet ought to be removed.

This may be called the paradox of poverty: Blessings ought not to be removed, and poverty is a blessing, yet it ought to be removed.

To try to clear up this mystery, I begin, as Socrates would, with some dull but necessary definitions.

1. A paradox is an apparent contradiction but not a real one.

2. A contradiction is the relationship between two propositions that exclude each other: if either is true, the other is false, and if either is false, the other is true.

3. Poverty is the opposite of wealth.

4. Different kinds of poverty are the opposites of different kinds of wealth. The two main kinds are material and spiritual wealth, and thus material and spiritual poverty.

5. Since money is designed as a means of exchange for all or nearly all material goods and services, economic poverty is identical, or nearly identical, with material poverty.

6. A clarification about spiritual poverty. Spiritual poverty is not the same as being "poor in spirit". Christ comes to *relieve* our spiritual poverty by removing our Original Sin and installing His sanctifying grace, which is received by the poor in spirit, the humble.

When Mother Teresa came to Harvard to give the commencement address, she began by criticizing the invitation Harvard had sent her. It had said something about inviting the most well-known citizen of one of the world's poorest countries to share her wisdom with the citizens of one of the world's richest countries. She said that was wrong. "It is something unbelievable that today a mother, herself, murders her own child. . . . This is one of the greatest poverties. A nation, people, family that allows that, that accepts that, they are the poorest of the poor."

The paradox of poverty does not emerge from our own thinking. It comes to us from God, from divine revelation (which is first of all Christ Himself, then, on His authority, His Church, and then, on her authority, her Scriptures). In one of the most well-known and well-loved passages in those Scriptures, we find the following paradox:

On the one hand, Christ tells us, in the very first of His "beatitudes", "Blessed are the poor."

On the other hand, we are commanded by that same authority (Christ, His Church, and her Scriptures) to minister to the needs of the poor, to relieve their poverty. The old term for this is "almsgiving". It is one of the three distinctive good works or marks of a Christian life, the other two being prayer and fasting.

These two truths seem to contradict each other. For if the poor are blessed, then when we deliver them from their poverty, we deliver them from their blessing—which is *not* a good work. And if it is a good work to deliver them from their poverty, then their poverty is not a blessing, for it is not good to take away another's blessing. To affirm that poverty is good (or "blessed") seems logically to imply that almsgiving is bad; and to affirm that almsgiving is good seems logically to imply that *poverty* is bad rather than blessed.

Since Christ is truth ("I am the way, the truth, and the life") and since truth, by definition, can never really contradict truth, this apparent contradiction cannot be a real one. It must be a paradox, an apparent contradiction.

Since a paradox is an apparent contradiction, and since saying that implies a knowledge of the distinction between an apparent contradiction and a real one, to say that this is a paradox implies that we know, or can know, how it is distinct from a real contradiction—or, in other words, that we can explain away the apparent contradiction in it.

So let's try to do just that.

The most easy and obvious way to explain away an apparent contradiction is to find a distinction. The most easy and obvious distinction here is between spiritual and material poverty. And this distinction seems to be the key to explaining the paradox because Christ Himself, when He says "blessed are the poor", explicitly specifies "the poor *in spirit*".

Now "the poor in spirit" cannot possibly mean "the spiritually poor". For Christ came precisely to relieve our spiritual poverty, which is essentially our sin, though He did not come for the express purpose of relieving our material poverty, which is essentially our economic poverty. God's angel announced that His name was to be "Jesus", or "Savior", not because He would save His people from their economic poverty or other sufferings, but because He would save His people from their sins.

This, by the way, was probably the misunderstanding that, more than any other, was responsible for His rejection by His own people, God's own chosen people and His collective prophet to the world. Their prophecies had identified the Messiah, God's Promised One, as the One Who would deliver Israel from its enemies. God had deliberately left the word "enemies" ambiguous in order to test the hearts of His readers. Those whose hearts were set above all on worldly goods, especially on wealth and power, identified their enemies as the Romans, who were depriving the Jews of wealth by their onerous taxation and of power by their tyrannical imperial occupation. These Jews did not recognize Jesus as their Savior because He did not save them from their material enemies. But those Jews who knew themselves and knew their God well enough to know that their real enemies were their own sins did recognize Him as their Savior.

By "Blessed are the poor in spirit", Christ could not possibly have meant "Blessed are those whose spirits are weak; blessed are the spiritual sissies." That is Nietzsche's profound misunderstanding of Christianity that led him to his profound hatred of it. Rather, Christ meant "Blessed are those whose spirits are *willing* to embrace the suffering of material poverty, whether their pockets and bank accounts are in fact poor or not." He meant: "Blessed are those whose hearts are detached from the wealth of this world so that they can be better attached to Me and to the wealth of My kingdom, which kingdom is not of this world but is the kingdom of Heaven, which is My reign in human hearts and lives, the reign of My *agape* love. Blessed are those who are in love with this love, for God is this love."

However, the distinction between spiritual and material poverty does not suffice to explain the paradox. For Christ was speaking only of material poverty when He said "Blessed are the poor", while the command actively to relieve others' poverty extends to both spiritual poverty *and* material poverty. It is true that spiritual poverty is far worse than material poverty, but we are to relieve both. So the paradox is still unresolved, since we are commanded to relieve the material poverty that Christ declares is a blessing.

He declares material poverty blessed in two ways: by saying exactly that and also by saying its obverse, that material wealth is spiritually dangerous. He did this on many occasions: for example, when he astonished His disciples by declaring that it was harder for a rich man to enter Heaven than for a camel to pass through the eye of a needle. However we interpret this, as literal, symbolical, allegorical, hyperbole, or reference to Jerusalem's "needle gate", the point is that wealth, like any kind of power, is dangerous (for "all power tends to corrupt"), which is one reason why material and economic poverty is blessed, whether this be poverty in external material fact or poverty in intention, in the heart's internal detachment from whatever worldly wealth one has, whether it is twopence or two palaces.

So we are left with the paradox that material poverty is a blessing and yet we are to relieve it.

Another solution is offered by Teilhard de Chardin in *The Divine Milieu*. It consists in distinguishing two temporal moments, during the first of which God wants us actively to relieve poverty and suffering, both of others and of ourselves, and during the second of which He wants us to accept our failures, our poverty, suffering, and death. These two moments are joined by what Teilhard calls an "anticipatory tendency" to accept failure even during the first phase. Here are his words:

> It is a perfectly correct view of things—and strictly consonant with the Gospel—to regard Providence across the ages as brooding over the world in ceaseless effort to spare that world its bitter wounds and to bind up its hurts. Most certainly it is God Himself who, in the course of the centuries, awakens the great benefactors of humankind, and the great physicians. . . Do not men acknowledge by instinct this divine presence when . . . they thank each one of those who have helped their body or their mind to freedom? . . . At the first approach of the diminishments we cannot hope to find God except by loathing what is coming upon us and doing our best to avoid it . . . without bitterness and without revolt, of course, but with an *anticipatory tendency* to acceptance and final resignation. (But) It is obviously difficult to separate the two 'instants . . .' without to some extent distorting them. . . .

What Teilhard says here is true, but it does not solve our problem. The problem with his solution is the same as the problem with the old Modernist theologians' solution to the problem that the Beatitudes are too perfect for us on earth: that therefore they must be meant for Heaven rather than for earth; or—a second version of the distinction—that they were meant only as an "interim ethic" for the period of time between the First and Second Comings, when

many of the early Christians believed that worldly posses-
sions were due to be swept away forever very shortly. A
third version of the same essential point is the solution that
is often associated, rightly or wrongly, with the Catholic
distinction between commands and counsels, or duties, and
actions *beyond* the call of duty: that the Beatitudes are for
the elite, the specially saintly, while the Commandments are
for the masses. The problem with all three of these distinctions is that the words of Christ, in the historical context in
which they were spoken, to ordinary people including His
disciples, neither speak of nor imply any such distinction of
two moments, either between the time in this world ver-
sus the time of Heaven (Teilhard's solution), between two
periods of time in this world (the Modernists' solution), or
between two classes of people (the old Catholic solution).
Rather, His words are addressed to everyone without distinction and to all times and occasions without distinction.
There is no restriction or qualification to them. That is why
they are so shocking. The three distinctions just mentioned
all misunderstand Christ because they make His words more
commonsensical and less shocking, while Christ is always
more shocking and less (apparently) commonsensical.

Perhaps the paradox can be explained by saying that the
poor tend to be more religious, thus more blessed. But then
why is it good to relieve their poverty? Poverty is like suffering—indeed, it is a form of suffering—and it is obviously
a Christlike thing to do to relieve our neighbors' suffering
when we can. Christ Himself did that, healing all sorts of
diseases and even raising the dead. This explains the second
part of our paradox, why we should relieve poverty, but not
the first, why poverty is blessed.

Sometimes we can solve a problem best by narrowing its
focus and then expanding the solution found there, rather

than broadening its focus and then applying the solution found there to the narrower topic. So let us try narrowing our focus from suffering in general to poverty and from poverty in general to poverty of money.

There is an illuminating reflection on money and wealth in C. S. Lewis' novel *Perelandra* that may help us. On an Eden-like planet called Perelandra, the protagonist discovers an almost irresistibly delicious bubble fruit. He drinks the liquid in one of them and then contemplates drinking more.

> Looking at a fine cluster of the bubbles which hung above his head he thought how easy it would be to get up and plunge oneself through the whole lot of them and to feel, all at once, that magical refreshment multiplied tenfold. But he was restrained by the same sort of feeling which had restrained him overnight from tasting a second gourd. He had always disliked the people who encored a favourite air in the opera—"That just spoils it" had been his comment. But this now appeared to him as a principle of far wider application and deeper moment. This itch to have things over again, as if life were a film that could be unrolled twice or even made to work backwards . . . was it possibly the root of all evil? No: of course the love of money was called that. But money itself—perhaps one valued it chiefly as a defence against chance, a security for being able to have things over again, as means of arresting the unrolling of the film. . . . Money, in fact, would provide the means of saying *encore* in a voice that could not be disobeyed.

The supreme "money", the supreme "encore", would be artificial immortality by genetic engineering. More on that later.

Perhaps we can unravel this paradox by the analogy between poverty and death. When we ask whether there is anything else that has this double aspect in Scripture, especially in Christ's own words, anything else that is both a blessing and something that it is blessed to be relieved of, we naturally think of death. Let's explore the parallel paradox regarding that.

Death is in objective fact the supreme suffering. It is not necessarily the most subjectively painful (most of us fear physical pain more than death), but it is the greatest objective loss, the loss of everything in this world. In death, we suffer the loss of everything in this life.

There is an old oratorio with the wonderfully paradoxical line: "Thou hast made death glorious and triumphant, for through its portals we enter into the presence of the living God." Death is at once "the last *enemy*" that Christ conquered in His Resurrection and also our only door to Heaven, our only hope. It is so necessary that if it were abolished by genetic engineering and artificial immortality, we would have Hell on earth. If you want a foretaste of that brave new world, just leave a dozen eggs out on your kitchen table for a year. As C. S. Lewis says, "We are like eggs at present. And you can not go on indefinitely being just an ordinary, decent egg. We must be hatched or go bad." (Yet this Hell is a project that a good number of geneticists not only see as possible but are actively working for. If they were to succeed, I think they would bring in the Great Tribulation and the Second Coming.)

What Christ did to death (the greatest objective suffering), He did to all other suffering, too, even its subjective dimension, pain. What did He do to it? The answer is my candidate for the greatest line in the history of cinema. In Mel Gibson's *The Passion of the Christ*, when Mary, on the *via dolorosa*, sees Him not just carrying His Cross but caressing it and cuddling it as a little boy does to his teddy bear, she asks Him, in uncomprehending agony, why He has to do all this, he replies, through His river of blood, sweat, and tears, "See, Mother, I make all things new."

He made death the door to a higher life. And therefore He also made suffering the key to a higher joy, when the suffering is endured with love and trust, since all suffering is a kind of death. And, therefore, He also made poverty blessed, since poverty is a kind of suffering. Suffering is a little death, and poverty is a little suffering; therefore, what applies to death also applies to suffering, and what applies to suffering also applies to poverty.

How does this work?

When He said, "Behold, I make all things new", did He really mean it? Did He mean *all* things? Did He mean poverty as well as suffering? Of course, since poverty is a kind of suffering. And did He mean suffering as well as death? Of course, since suffering the loss of any good is a kind of death, and in death we suffer the loss of all material goods, even our own body.

And what about sin? If He makes all things new and even "everything . . . works for good", as St. Paul boldly claims in Romans 8:28, does He do that to sins, too? Not in the same way, no. But in some real, new way, yes. Judas Iscariot's betrayal, the most awful deed in history, helped bring about our salvation, though not his. Even the Devil's success in killing God Incarnate, apparently splitting the divine Trinity, at least in consciousness, when Christ uttered those most awful words ever spoken ("My God, my God, why have you forsaken me?"), when God was forsaken of God and God Himself seemed to become for a second almost an atheist—this greatest triumph of Hell was what won for us Heaven. This greatest of all sins and this greatest of all

sufferings is what Christians commemorate and even cele-
brate on a day they call "*Good* Friday". And even our own
sins, through the golden door of repentance, though only
through that door, can be made to work together for good
if only we trust Him and love Him. That's what the startling
verse, Romans 8:28, says.

That is the ultimate solution to the atheist's strongest argument, the problem of evil. That is why God allows any evils,
physical or spiritual: always for some greater good. Augustine says: "The Almighty . . . would never permit . . . anything evil among His works if He were not so omnipotent
and good that He can bring good even out of evil." Even
Adam's sin Augustine called "*felix culpa*", "happy fault", because it brought about such a great redemption. But no man
of Adam's time, the time before Christ, could foresee what
He would do in Christ, and no man in Christ's time, or in
the time after Christ, our time, can foresee what He will
do in the end, when He restores all things in Christ. Eye
has not seen, ear has not heard, nor has it entered into the
heart of any man, not even the greatest saints and mystics,
the things God has prepared for those who love Him. That
is the only full and total solution to the problem of evil:
God's solution, not ours.

Once we dare to enter these far greater precincts, the
problem of poverty looks tiny and the problem of reconcil-
ing the paradox of poverty looks almost easy. The problem
is not so much solved as dissolved, as most of our questions
will be on the Last Day, the Parousia. Job forgot every one
of his questions, his excellent, deep, honest, passionate, and
agonizing questions, when God simply showed His face and
asked Job the great and gloriously unanswerable question:
Who are you? Were you there when the morning stars sang
together as My angels and I designed you and your world?

Job's answer was simple: "Now I know who you are and who I am. I had heard about you with the hearing of the ear, but now I see you with the seeing of the eye, and I repent in dust and ashes. For now I know who I am: I am the man who filled my mouth with empty-headed words."

That is also pretty much what the world's greatest theologian said about the world's greatest work of theology, when St. Thomas Aquinas, having been graced with a glimpse of the Face Job saw, declared that everything he had ever written, including the unfinished *Summa*, was "straw". In the Middle Ages, straw was used to cover animal dung, the very thing Job sat on: a "dung heap". Not since King James has any Bible translator dared to translate that word literally.

The point is obvious: God knows what poverties, sufferings, diseases, and deaths are good for us, but we do not. If we did, we would be as wise as God, so that if we *could* answer the atheist's strongest argument, the problem of evil, this would prove, not theism, but atheism; it would prove that there is no mind above our own. Our *inability* to solve the problem of evil is exactly what the hypothesis of theism entails; the existence of unexplainable evil confirms rather than disconfirms the existence of God. It certainly does not disprove it.

Boethius makes this point in *The Consolation of Philosophy* about the contrast between divine omniscience and human ignorance as the solution to why divine providence seems so irrational and random to us if in fact God always works everything together for our good:

> Even though things may seem confused and discordant to you, because you cannot discern the order that governs them, nevertheless everything is governed by its own proper order directing all things toward the good. . . . Therefore when you see something happen here contrary to

your ideas of what is right, it is your opinion and expectation which is confused, while the order of things themselves is right.

Take, for example, the man so fortunate as to seem approved by . . . God . . . he may actually be so weak in character that if he were to suffer adversity he would forsake virtue on the grounds that it seemed not to bring him good fortune. Therefore God in his wise dispensation spares the man whom adversity might ruin. . .

Another man who is perfect in all virtues, holy, and dear to God, may be spared . . . because Providence judges it wrong for him to be touched by any adversity. . . .

To others, Providence gives a mixture of prosperity and adversity according to the disposition of their souls: she gives trouble to some whom too much luxury might spoil; others she tests with hardships in order to strengthen their virtues by the exercise of patience. . . . Some . . . by not breaking under torture, have proved to the world that virtue cannot be conquered by evil. . . .

Moreover, the lot of the wicked, which is sometimes painful and sometimes easy, comes from the same source and for the same reasons. No one wonders at the troubles they undergo, since everyone thinks that is just what they deserve. Such punishment both deters others from crime and prompts those who suffer it to reform. On the other hand, the prosperity of the wicked is a powerful argument for the good, because they see how they ought to evaluate the kind of good fortune which the wicked so often enjoy. Still another good purpose may be served by the prosperity of the wicked man: if his nature is so reckless and violent that poverty might drive him to crime.

These imagined examples of Boethius are only "perhapses", not definitive answers to the problem of evil, not documents leaked from the War Room in Heaven. They only open our minds and imaginations to possibilities and, therefore, to the possibility that our faith in the perfection of divine providence is intellectually respectable and compatible with the puzzling and apparently random data.

As C. S. Lewis says in *A Grief Observed*, his personal diary about the suffering of his wife who had just died of cancer, "But is it credible that such extremities of torture should be necessary for us? Well, take your choice. The tortures occur. If they are unnecessary, then there is no God or a bad one. If there is a good God, then these tortures are necessary. For no even moderately good Being could possibly inflict or permit them if they weren't."

Here is how Lewis explains the paradox of poverty in *The Problem of Pain* (chap. 7). Both his statement of the problem and his solution are shorter and clearer than mine, so please do not pardon me but thank me for giving you a three-paragraph-long quotation from the most clear and intelligent Christian writer of modern times:

> There is a paradox about tribulation in Christianity. Blessed are the poor, but by 'judgement' (i.e., social justice) and alms we are to remove poverty wherever possible. Blessed are we when persecuted, but we may avoid persecution . . . and may pray to be spared it, as Our Lord prayed in Gethsemane. But if suffering is good, ought it not to be pursued rather than avoided? I answer that suffering [including poverty] is not good in itself. What is good in any painful experience is, for the sufferer, his submission to the will of God, and, for the spectators, the compassion aroused and the acts of mercy to which it leads. In the fallen and partially redeemed universe we may distinguish (1) the simple good descending from God, (2) the simple evil produced by rebellious creatures, and (3) the exploitation of that evil by God for His redemptive purpose, which produces (4) the complex good to which accepted suffering and repented sin contribute. . . .

A merciful man aims at his neighbour's good and so does 'God's will', consciously co-operating with the 'simple good'. A cruel man oppresses his neighbour, and so does simple evil. But in doing such evil, he is used by God, without his own knowledge or consent, to produce the complex good—so that the first man serves God as a son, and the second as a tool. For you will certainly carry out God's purpose, however you act, but it makes a difference to you whether you serve like Judas or like John. . . .

It would be quite false, therefore, to suppose that the Christian view of suffering [and poverty—that it is blessed when accepted in trusting love] is incompatible with the strongest emphasis on our duty to leave the world, even in a temporal sense, 'better' than we found it. In the fullest parabolic picture which He gave of the Judgment, Our Lord seems to reduce all virtue to active beneficence: and though it would be misleading to take that one picture in isolation from the Gospel as a whole, it is sufficient to place beyond doubt the basic principle of the social ethics of Christianity.

Lewis is, of course, a "conservative" because he wants to conserve everything that comes from Christ. But is it not wonderful that both the so-called liberal Christian and the so-called conservative Christian must agree on this practical bottom line? And is it not wonderful that in fact they do agree about this end, the relief of poverty, however strongly they disagree about the means, especially about the relation between the roles of government and of private initiative as means to this end? Christians, unlike Muslims, do not believe that God has revealed the best political system, so we have been arguing about that for 2000 years and will continue to do so. Divine revelation is given to us on a need-to-know basis. And we are told much more about our orthopraxy than about our orthodoxy; about what we are to do than about why we are to do it. That is why orthopraxy leads to orthodoxy, why one of the most effective means to attaining right faith is right charity. In other words, we will solve our remaining disputes only in proportion as we become saints. That is the most powerful solution to all social and political and even economic problems. Two more Mother Teresas would do more for the health and happiness of our poor world than ten FDRs or JFKs, and more than ten Maggie Thatchers or ten Ronald Reagans. So what's your excuse for not being one of them?

5

The Logic of Liberalism

1. Today's ideas are truer than yesterday's ideas. Of course, they will be yesterday's ideas tomorrow.

2. Discriminating people don't discriminate.

3. Extremism is extremely bad.

4. Don't trust words.

5. Throughout history, there has never been a Utopia. Therefore, history proves that there will be one soon.

6. Forbidding things is forbidden. You shouldn't ever say "shouldn't".

7. You may worship any God but God.

8. All other cultures are right except Western culture. All other cultures believe that Western culture is wrong in believing that all cultures are right. Therefore all other cultures are right except Western culture.

9. The Hell with Hell. People who believe in damnation should be damned. The idea that some ideas are damnable ideas is a damnable idea.

10. There is no truth. And that's the truth.

11. Absolutely no absolutes.

12. Men and women are the same. Especially women.

13. There are no universal truths. Not anywhere.

14. You can be certain that all claims to certainty are arrogant nonsense.

15. The Catholic Church has done only one thing right. In 1966, she put the *Index of Forbidden Books* on the Index. Censorship should be censored.

16. I can't tolerate any intolerance.

17. Manifestos are intolerant. We need to get rid of all manifestos. This is a manifesto.

18. Love sins, hate sinners. Saints say they are sinners. Hate them. Sinners say they are saints. Love them.

19. We must be very religious about having no religion.

20. Spirituality is good, but religion is dangerous because it believes in things like spirits.

21. Invest in the future. It's the only dimension of time that doesn't exist.

22. We have a right to clean air because we have a right to breathe dirty words.

23. The government knows best, unless it's a government elected by people who don't vote for people like us.

24. The government knows what's best for the people better than do the people who elected us.

25. Judgmentalism is a very bad thing.

26. Don't be negative.

27. All men are equal except those who think some are superior.

28. Conserve the environment, but don't be conservative.

29. There is no infallible institution in this world. This must be true because the ACLU says so.

30. All reasoning is only rationalizing. And that's not just rationalizing.

31. Abolish capital punishment. Capital punishment kills killers. But abortion is OK, because that kills only the innocent. If we labeled the unborn as killers, we could abolish abortion by abolishing capital punishment.

32. Actually, there's no inconsistency in being against capital punishment and for abortion, since capital punishment kills killers, and abortionists are killers, and pro-abortionists certainly don't want abortionists killed.

33. The proletariat will save the world—by voting for rich liberals.

34. Trust the experts (us). You need us because you need our superior wisdom. Our superior wisdom says there is no such thing as superior wisdom.

35. All philosophies are culturally relative. All are blinded by their cultural limitations. Except that one.

36. Everyone is prejudiced except us.

37. Trust us. We are your servants. We will spend your money for you.

38. There is nothing eternal. Ever.

39. There is no "meaning of life". That's the meaning of life.

40. All life's problems are solved by economics. But the love of money is the root of all evil. Don't be a capitalist.

41. Deconstructionism, the "state of the art" literary theory, means that a book can mean anything you want it to mean—unless you want it to mean what the author wanted it to mean.

42. "All men are created equal." But "all" is stereotyping.

And "men" is gender-exclusive (even though everyone who ever used it for 1000 years meant by it "male *and* female human beings").

And "are" is dogmatic.

And "created" is religious (spit! cough!). And "equal" is a substitute for sugar.

43. There are only two kinds of people: those who are so simplistic that they think there are only two kinds of people, and those who are broad-minded like us.

44. "Do I contradict myself? Very well then I contradict myself. (I am large, I contain multitudes.)" (Walt Whitman, "Song of Myself"). And therefore, since I contradict myself, I am small, I contain nothing.

45. "Consistency is the hobgoblin of little minds." And therefore, to be consistently inconsistent, it isn't.

46. We are better than you are because we don't believe that we are better than you are.

47. The Far Left and the Far Right are totally opposite. You can see it in the pictures: Stalin had a much better mustache than Hitler.

48. There is no such thing as "Far Left". There is only Far Right. In fact, all Right is Far Right.

49. The idea that all ideas are equal is equal to the idea that not all ideas are equal, if all ideas are equal.

50. Be open-minded to all ideas. But not to the idea that perhaps you should not be open-minded to *all* ideas.

51. I love all human beings. I hate only conservatives.

52. We should be totally free, free to contradict ourselves. And therefore we shouldn't be.

53. There are no absolutes. Except sex.

54. There's no "objective truth", just personal opinions. And that's not just a personal opinion.

55. We hate censorship. We love speech codes.

56. Good skeptics place limits to thought and do not claim to think beyond those limits. But to *think* a limit, you have to think both sides of that limit.

57. Never say "never".

58. Our ancestors were apes, and we will teach our descendants to believe that about us too.

59. The idea of "heresies" is a heresy.

60. Logic is a fake. It's a dead white male chauvinist plot to rape the minds of women. And I'll prove it.

61. Negate all negativity.

62. We respect anyone who does not respect us.

63. Everything is relative. A bird is only an egg's clever *way* of making more eggs.

64. The idea of superiority is a very inferior idea.

65. Don't trust anyone else's philosophy. That's my philosophy, and you can trust it.

66. I believe we should believe only what's been proved. But I can't prove that.

67. "Sola Scientia" is like "sola Scriptura". It says that you can be certain only of what Science has proved. But Science hasn't proved that.

68. How shall we think rightly about orthodoxies? ("Orthodoxy" means "right thinking".) Here's how: All orthodoxies are dangerous things. That's our orthodoxy.

69. Our reasoning is only the rationalizing of our animal desires and brain chemistry. It takes reason to see through the popular superstition that reason is anything more than that.

70. There are many ways of understanding the Koran. And they are all valid. Except for the Koranic one.

71. We believe what we believe only because Society has conditioned us to believe it. And Society has conditioned us to believe *that*. Some people don't believe that, though. So society must have conditioned them to believe that Society doesn't condition them. So Society lies.

72. The difference between Science and Religion is that Science abandons ideas that are irrational, especially ideas that are logically self-contradictory, while Religion stubbornly keeps believing them and calls unbelievers wrong. And if you don't believe *that*, you're wrong.

73. Only inferior people believe that some people are superior to others.

74. We are humane. We are compassionate. We believe that pain is the only evil. And therefore we approve crushing the skulls of half-born babies and jabbing scissors into the back of their necks.

75. It's bad to be good, and it's good to be bad. For goodness is dull conformity, but badness is creative nonconformity. In fact, the only thing that's bad is goodness. Everything else is OK. And the only thing that's good is badness. Everything else is conformity.

76. Conform to nonconformity.

77. Conservatives don't believe there is any such thing as *subjective* truth, a truth that's true for one person but not for another. That belief is true for them but not for us.

78. "I believe truth is objective." "Well, that's true for you."

79. "I believe it's impossible for one person to 'impose' truth on another." "How dare you impose your personal belief on me?"

80. We are so open-minded and tolerant and unprejudiced that if you disagree with us, you must be very closed-minded and intolerant and prejudiced. And your hairdo is stupid looking, too.

81. "There is nothing good or bad, but thinking makes it so." Therefore, if I think that there is something good or bad that is not made good or bad by thinking, my thinking will make *that* so, too.

82. Egalitarians are superior to elitists.

83. "For the *New York Times*, the only good Catholic is a bad Catholic" (Fr. Neuhaus).

84. "It is better to travel hopefully than to arrive." And, therefore, we can only hope never to arrive.

85. Everything changes, even the standards of measurement. We don't use iron yardsticks. We use eels.

86. We believe in progress, and we don't believe in unchanging goals. So the station is moving as fast as the train. That's progress.

87. "Question authority." And say that authoritatively.

88. All cultures are right except ours. Ours is the only one that believes that all cultures are right.

89. Nothing is forbidden here. Don't you dare bring in some repressive Law!

90. "Everybody's opinion is true. No opinion is simply wrong." "But some people have the opinion that not everybody's opinion is true." "They're wrong."

This is getting tiresome, so I'll let you fill in the rest.

6

The Social, Moral, and Sexual
Effects of Symbolic Logic

When I started teaching logic, in 1962, most of the text-books taught traditional Aristotelian logic rather than the (then still fairly new) "symbolic logic", also called "mathematical logic" or "propositional calculus". Sixty years later, there are only two full-length texts of traditional Aristotelian logic in print. One of them is my own recently published logic textbook, *Socratic Logic*,[1] from which much of the middle part of this article is taken. All the other logic texts, over five hundred of them, teach symbolic logic or else informal logic (rhetoric).

By the seventies, most of the English-speaking philosophical establishment had cast its lot with "analytic philosophy" and the symbolic logic that was its methodological complement. I still vividly remember the reaction of outrage, fear, and loathing that came from that establishment when Henry Veatch published *The Two Logics*,[2] his attack on the new logic. The book was a bit verbose, bombastic, and intemperate, but it possessed the three rarest and most important qualities any book of philosophy should have: it was

---

[1] Peter Kreeft, *Socratic Logic: A Logic Text Using Socratic Method, Platonic Questions and Aristotelian Principles* (South Bend, Ind.: St. Augustine's Press, 2003).

[2] Henry B. Veatch, *Two Logics: The Conflict between Classical and Neo-analytic Philosophy* (Evanston, Ill. Northwestern University, 1969).

interesting, it was rational, and it was right. That's why the establishment "went postal". People will forgive you for being wrong, but they will never forgive you for being right.

But this change in logic is not just a technical, in-house issue for philosophers. It concerns everyone, and it has serious social, moral, and even sexual implications, and it is one of the unrecognized indirect causes of "the culture of death", as I shall try to show.

A Prophetic Phone Call

I realized this only reluctantly. What first buzzed my inner alarm was a phone call I received years ago from a man who was quite famous (but not with me: I have forgotten his name). He had written a book attacking the computer revolution. The book had been on the *New York Times* best-seller list for a number of weeks and had elicited high praise. He had been called "one of the ten most intelligent men in the world". He thought he had found in me an ally for his cyber-Luddite philosophy because he had read some personal complaint against computers in one of my books. (Yes, I do hate the arrogant little bastards. They are robbers, tricksters, and snobs. "I hate them with perfect hatred, I count them my enemies.") This author tried to persuade me of the following apocalyptic scenario: the use of computers, he claimed, was imperceptibly changing the very structure of human thought into a geometrically increasing left-brain dominance and right-brain atrophy; so that as we became more and more willing servants of more and more elaborate calculating machines, our acts of ordinary intuitive understanding were becoming rarer and harder. He seemed to me extremist and a conspiracy theorist, and I mentally labeled him a crank and a crackpot. But he offered me three pieces of empirically verifiable evidence for his hypothesis, each of them testable by anyone who had taught logic for decades.

The first was the general prediction that students would become increasingly incapacitated in Aristotelian logic as they became increasingly capable in symbolic logic. The second was more specific: that they would be increasingly unable to understand analogies and analogical terms. (For understanding analogies is one thing digital computers cannot do. It is an intuitive, "right-brain" act.) The third prediction was the most specific of all and, I thought, the most absurd: the Scholastic Aptitude Test (SAT) taken by nearly every applicant to college in America would soon abolish its entire section on analogies because upcoming students would no longer be able to understand them. (These tests had not been substantively changed in fifty years, though they had been repeatedly "dumbed down".)

A few years later, the third prediction literally came true.

Remembering the other predictions, I got out some of my oldest, easiest logic tests, from 1962, and gave them to my present logic students. They failed quite spectacularly, especially the questions about analogical terms. For instance, only three students in a class of seventy-five understood that in the sentence "He pointed with his right hand to the hands of the clock", the word "hands" is analogical. Very few had any trouble with that in 1962.

But this is only a change in abstract logical thinking; where are the social, moral, and sexual consequences that this chapter title claims?

In order for me to explain this, I need to give you a very short course in the history of logic and modern philosophy.

A Short History of the Rise of Symbolic Logic

About 350 years before Christ, Aristotle wrote the world's first logic textbook. It was actually six books, which collectively came to be known as the *Organon*, or "instrument". From then until 1913, when Bertrand Russell and Alfred North Whitehead published *Principia Mathematica*, the world's first classic of mathematical or symbolic logic, all students in all universities in the world learned Aristotelian logic. The only other "new logic" for twenty-four centuries had been a seventeenth-century improvement on the principles of inductive logic and scientific method by Francis Bacon, the *Novum Organum* ("new Organon"), and another by John Stuart Mill in the nineteenth century. But today, "logic" virtually *means* "symbolic logic".

There are at least three good reasons *for* the current triumph of symbolic logic over Aristotelian logic. But each comes at a price.

The first and most obvious one is that the new logic really is superior to the old in efficiency for expressing long and complex arguments, much as Arabic numerals are superior to Roman numerals, or a digital computer to an analog computer, or writing in shorthand to writing in longhand.

However, longhand is superior to shorthand in other ways: for instance, it has more beauty and elegance, it is intelligible to more people, and it gives a more personal touch. That is why it is more useful for beginners. That is why most people write in longhand. It is similar in logic: most people "argue in longhand", that is, ordinary language, and Aristotelian logic stays close to ordinary language. That is why it is more useful for beginners.

A second reason for preferring symbolic logic is its more exact, scientific form. Symbolic logic is *mathematical* logic. "Modern symbolic logic has been developed primarily by

mathematicians with mathematical applications in mind",
says one of its defenders, Henry C. Byerly.[3] Mathematics
is a wonderful invention for saving time and empowering
science, but it is not very useful in ordinary or philosophical conversations. In fact, the more important the subject
matter, the less useful mathematics seems to be. Its forte is
not quality but quantity. It is the only totally clear, totally
unambiguous language in the world, but it cannot say anything very interesting about anything very important.

The philosophical god of symbolic logicians, Ludwig
Wittgenstein himself, admitted in his *Philosophical Investi-
gations* that "because of the basic differences between natural and artificial languages, often such translations [from
natural-language sentences into artificial symbolic language]
are not even possible in principle." That is why Stephen N.
Thomas said, in 1973, that "many logicians now agree that
the methods of symbolic logic are of little practical useful-
ness in dealing with much reasoning encountered in real-life
situations."[4]

—And in philosophy! "However helpful symbolic logic
may be as a tool of the . . . sciences, it is useless as a tool of
philosophy. Philosophy aims at insight into principles and
into the relationship of conclusions to the principles from
which they are derived. Symbolic logic, however, does not
aim at giving such insight." This from Andrew Bachhuber's
Introduction to Logic.[5]

There is a third reason for the triumph of symbolic logic
among philosophers, and this one is philosophical or ideological. Aristotelian logic was scorned by most twentieth-

[3] Henry C. Byerly, *A Primer of Logic* (New York: Harper & Row, 1973).

[4] Stephen N. Thomas, *Practical Reasoning in Natural Language* (Englewood
Cliffs, N.J.: Prentice-Hall, 1973).

[5] Andrew H. Bachhuber, *Introduction to Logic* (New York: Appleton-Cen-
tury-Crofts, 1957).

century philosophers because it rests on two unfashionable, though commonsensical, philosophical assumptions. The technical terms for them are "epistemological realism" and "metaphysical realism". These two assumptions were believed by nearly all philosophers for nearly two thousand years (roughly, from Socrates until the eighteenth century), and they are still believed by most ordinary people today, but *not* by most of the influential philosophers of the twentieth century. The first assumption, epistemological realism, says that the object of human reason, when reason is working naturally and rightly, is objective reality; that human reason can know things as they really are and can sometimes know them with certainty; that when we say, "Two apples plus two apples must always be four apples" or "Apples grow on trees", we are saying something true about the universe, not just about how we think or use symbols.

There are two main reasons many twentieth-century philosophers were skeptical of this belief: in two words, Hume and Kant, the two most influential eighteenth-century "Enlightenment" philosophers.

David Hume inherited from his empiricist predecessor John Locke the fatal assumption that the immediate object of human knowledge is our own ideas. Locke had naïvely assumed that we could know that these ideas "corresponded" to objective reality, somewhat like photos; but it is difficult to know how we can be sure any photo accurately corresponds to the real object of which it is a photo if the only things we can ever know directly are photos and not real objects. Hume drew the logical conclusion of skepticism from Locke's premise.

Once he limited the objects of knowledge to our own ideas, Hume then distinguished two kinds of ideas, which he called "(sense) impressions" and "ideas" (in the narrow sense), and two corresponding kinds of knowledge, which

he called "matters of fact" and "relations of ideas". By "relations of ideas", he meant basically what Kant later called
"analytic propositions" or what logicians call "tautologies":
propositions that are true by definition, true by form rather
than content, true only because their predicate merely repeats all or part of their subject—for example, "Trees are
trees", or "Unicorns are not non-unicorns", or "Unmarried
men are men."

On the other hand, by "matters of fact", Hume meant
basically what Kant later called "synthetic propositions",
propositions whose predicate adds some new information
to the subject—for example, "Some trees never shed their
leaves", or "No Englishman is twenty-five feet tall." Hume
argued that this kind of proposition can be known only by
sense observation. They are always particular, like "These
two men are bald", rather than universal, like "All men are
mortal", for we do not *sense* universals like "all men", only
particulars like "these two men".

Common sense tells us that we can be certain of some universal truths, like "All men are mortal", and that we can be
certain of the particular conclusions we validly deduce from
them, like "Socrates is mortal." But, according to Hume,
we can *not* be certain of universal truths because the only
way we can come to know them is by generalizing from
particular sense experiences; and since we cannot sense all
men, we cannot be certain that all men are mortal.

Since these general principles can only be probable, the
particular conclusions we deduce from them can only be
probable. If it is only probably true that all men are mortal,
it is only probably true that Socrates is mortal.

Hume's conclusion from this analysis was skeptical: there
is no certain knowledge of the real world ("matters of fact"),
only of tautologies ("relations of ideas"). Even science lacks

certainty, because science assumes the general principle of causality, and this principle, according to Hume, is not a universal objective truth but only a subjective association of ideas in our mind. Because we have seen a "constant conjunction" of birds and eggs, because we have so often seen eggs follow birds in time, we naturally assume that birds *cause* eggs. But we do not *see* causality itself, we see only birds and eggs. We do not *see* universals, and we do not *see* the universal principle that effects come from causes. So, Hume concluded, we do not really have the knowledge of objective reality that we naturally believe we have. We must be skeptics, if we are only Humean beings.

Immanuel Kant accepted most of Hume's epistemological analysis but said, in effect, "I Kant accept your skeptical conclusion." He thought he avoided this conclusion by denying the assumption that human reason is *supposed to* conform to objective reality and fails to do its job. Kant said, instead, that human reason's job is to *form* or *construct* its object, as an artist forms or constructs his art. The knowing subject determines the known object rather than vice versa. Human reason does its job quite well, but its job is not to *discover* what is but to *make* it, to shape it, to structure it, to impose form on matter, unconsciously and ubiquitously. Kant distinguished three such levels of structuring: the two "forms of perception", space and time; twelve abstract logical "categories" such as causality, necessity, substance, and relation; and three "ideas of pure reason", God, self, and world.

Thus the world of experience is determined by our knowing it rather than our knowing being determined by the world. Kant called this idea his "Copernican revolution in philosophy". It is also called "epistemological idealism" or, more properly, "Kantian idealism". ("Epistemological idealism" is sometimes used in a broader sense to mean the belief that ideas rather than objective realities are the objects of our knowledge; in that sense, Locke and Hume are also epistemological idealists.)

The "bottom line" for logic is that if you agree with either Hume or Kant, logic becomes the mere manipulation of our symbols, not the principles for a true and orderly knowledge of an ordered world. Categories like "relation" or "quality" or "substance", and perhaps even "time" and "self" and "God", are not real features of the world we discover, only mental classifications we make.

In such a logic, "genus" and "species" mean only any larger class and smaller sub-classes that we mentally construct. But in Aristotelian logic, a "genus" is the general, common, or universal part of a thing's real essential nature— for example, "animal" is man's "genus". And a "species" is the whole essence—for example, "rational animal" is man's "species". So for Aristotle, a genus is part of (the internal meaning of) a species rather than a species being part of (the external population of) a genus.

This involves the second commonsensical Aristotelian assumption, metaphysical realism, which is the belief that essences, or universals (like "man", "animal", or "substance"), are objectively real. The two assumptions are mutual corollaries: epistemological realism says that the object of human reason (of conceptual intelligence and not just sense perception) is objective reality; while metaphysical realism says that objective reality includes the objects of human conceptual intelligence (that is, universals). Epistemological realism says that intelligence knows reality, and metaphysical realism says that reality is intelligible; that it is ordered; that when we say "Man is a rational animal", we are not imposing an order on a reality that is really unknowable, formless, random, or chaotic; that universal categories are taken from reality into thought and language, not imposed on reality from thought and language.

(There are two versions of metaphysical realism. Plato believed that universals were real *things* in themselves, while Aristotle believed, more commonsensically, that they were real *aspects* of things that we mentally abstracted from things.)

The opposite of metaphysical realism is *nominalism*, the belief that universals are only *names (nomini)*. William of Ockham (1285–1347) is the philosopher who is usually credited (or debited) with being the founder of nominalism. G. K. Chesterton refuted nominalism with his usual economy and wit when he argued, "If [as the nominalist says] all chairs were quite different you could not call them 'all chairs'?"[6]

Aristotelian logic assumes both epistemological realism and metaphysical realism because it begins with "the first act of the mind", the act of understanding a universal, a nature, or an essence, such as the nature of "apple" or "man". These universals, essences, or natures are known by *concepts* and expressed by what logic calls *terms*. Then, in "the second act of the mind", the act of judgment, two of these terms are related as subject and predicate of a proposition—for example, "Apples are fruits" or "All men are mortal." And in "the third act of the mind", the act of reasoning, a further proposition (the "conclusion") is deduced from two previous propositions (the "premises")—for example, "All men are mortal and Socrates is a man, therefore Socrates is mortal."

[6] G. K. Chesterton, *Orthodoxy*, in *Collected Works*, vol. 1 (San Francisco: Ignatius Press, 1986), 238.

"Aristotle never intended his logic to be a merely for-mal calculus (like mathematics). He tied logic to his on-tology (metaphysics): thinking in concepts presupposes that the world is formed of stable species."[7]

Symbolic logic, in contrast, is a set of symbols and rules for manipulating them without needing to know their mean-ing and content or their relationship to the real world, their "truth" (in the traditional, commonsensical sense of "truth"). A computer can do symbolic logic. It is purely quantitative, not qualitative. It is digital, it is reducible to zero-sum mathematics.

Symbolic logic is also called "propositional logic" because it begins with propositions, not with terms. For terms like "man", "apple", or "mortal" express universals, essences, or natures; and to admit that these are real would admit the reality of universals (metaphysical realism) and that we can know them as they are (epistemological realism).

Typically modern philosophers criticize that assumption as naïve, but it seems to me a very reasonable assumption and not naïve at all. Is it naïve to assume that we know what an apple is? I would not want to go to your house for lunch if you really believe that you do not know what an apple is.

Symbolic logic has no way of knowing and prevents us from saying *what* anything is! But that was the essential Socratic question about everything. Symbolic logic would make Socrates impossible.

The very nature of reason itself is understood differently by symbolic logic from the way it was by Aristotelian logic. The ancients used "reason" to mean all that distinguished man from the beasts, including intuition, understanding, wisdom, moral conscience, and aesthetic appreciation as well

---

[7] Robert Lenoble, *Essai sur la notion d'expérience* (Paris: Vrin, 1943).

as calculation. But beginning with Descartes, it is only the last of these powers that we think of when we think of "reason". That is why there are philosophers today who actually believe there is no fundamental difference between "natural intelligence" and "artificial intelligence", that is, between humans and computers. In other words, man is nothing but an ape plus a computer. Having met some of these philosophers at Harvard and MIT, I must admit that their self-description sometimes seems quite accurate.

The Cultural Consequences

The new logic is like Orwell's "Newspeak" in *1984*: it shrinks language rather than expanding it. In it, we can no longer ask the Socratic question of the "what", the essence. If we cease to say a thing, we soon cease to think it, for there will be no holding-places in our language for the thought. Language is the house of thought, and homelessness is as life-threatening for thoughts as it is for people. If we should begin to speak and think only in nominalistic terms, that would be a monumental historic change. It would be the reversal of the evolutionary event by which man rose above the animal in gaining the ability to know abstract universals. It would be the mental equivalent of going naked on all fours, living in trees, and eating bugs and bananas. (Could monkeys have evolved by natural selection from nominalists?)

While it may seem "extremist" to suggest it, such a mental "devolution" is not impossible. And the use of computers is not unrelated to it. Already, "internet logic", the logic of spontaneous association by "keywords", is replacing genus and species logic, the logic of an ordered hierarchy of objectively real categories that express natural essences. In fact, to most modern minds, the last seven nouns and adjectives of that sentence already seem as archaic as alchemy or feudalism. And those that do understand them often label them ideologically dangerous. They contend that classifications like "Hittites" and universal statements about classes like "Hittites could not read Hebrew" constitute stereotyping, judgmentalism, prejudice, oppression, or even "hate speech".

Logic and social change are not unrelated. (Logic is not unrelated to *anything*.) Our society no longer thinks about the fundamental metaphysical question, the question of *what* something is, the question of the "nature" of a thing. Instead, we think about how we feel about things, how we can use them, how they work, how we can change them, how we see them behave, and how we can predict and control their behavior by technology. But none of this raises us above the animal level in kind, only in degree. The higher animals, too, have feelings about things, use things, understand how some things work and how they can change them, see them behave, and can predict and even control their behavior by a kind of primitive technology. For the act of hunting is technological; it is an art of predicting and controlling the behavior of other animals. What does man have that no other animal has? The very thing that is vilified by many modern philosophers: abstract concepts. We can abstract and understand universals. That is the power on which Aristotelian logic is founded, and that is the thing symbolic logic ignores or denies.

The old logic was like the old classic movies: strong on substance rather than on sophistication. The new logic is like the typically modern movies: strong on "special effects" but weak on substance, on theme, character, plot, and language;

strong on "bells and whistles" but weak on the engine; strong on the technological side but weak on the human side. But logic should be a human instrument. Logic was made for man, not man for logic.

The Ethical and Sexual Consequences

Symbolic logic is essentially a logic of "if . . . then . . . ", a logic of antecedent and consequent propositions; and it is a mathematical logic, a logic of quantity. These two features perfectly fit and foster utilitarianism in ethics because utilitarianism is essentially an ethics of "if . . . then . . . ", an ethics of consequences; and it is also an ethics of quantity. For its fundamental principle is that an act is ethically good if its foreseeable consequences constitute "the greatest happiness for the greatest number". (This is a version of "the end justifies the means", though that formula is somewhat ambiguous.)

In contrast, Aristotelian logic naturally fits and fosters a natural law ethics because its basic unit is a term that expresses a nature or essence, and its basic judgment is "All S is P", which is a statement of universal truth or law about the nature or quality of S (as expressed in P). It is essentially a logic of natures, of universal kinds and categories, of qualities and essences, and the principles of natural law ethics are based on and abstracted from the universal nature of man.

Before symbolic logic, Western culture, despite its pluralism and creativity, displayed a strong, deeply rooted, nearly universal, and rarely questioned consensus—and not just a consensus but an understanding—about most of the basic aspects of the universal natural moral law, about what was natural and what was unnatural to man. There probably was not a greater *obedience* to this law in the past, but there certainly was a much greater *knowledge* of it and *belief* in it.

By far the most radically changed area of morality in both belief and practice is sex. We routinely speak of "the sexual *revolution*". We do not use that word for any other aspect of ethical change. For today, most people find the traditional language about "unnatural acts" not only politically incorrect and offensive, but literally incomprehensible. This is because they no longer accept the legitimacy of the very question of the "nature" of a human act—the thing symbolic logic disallows. Who today still debates issues like homosexuality, contraception, masturbation, divorce, adultery, or even incest, pedophilia, and bestiality, in terms of the "nature" of sexuality, the "nature" of femininity and masculinity, and the "nature" of marriage? Traditional Roman Catholics and Evangelicals. No one else. It is not a far-fetched suspicion that the most powerful force driving the new logic is more sexual than logical.

I will therefore conclude with a prediction, in the spirit of my prophetic phone call. I predict that when the sexual wisdom of John Paul II's "theology of the body" becomes better known and more widely accepted, there will also be a restoration of Aristotelian logic.

7

Twelve Core Values

I was asked to talk about the twelve core values of the Lumen Institute. But how? I could have said a little bit about each one or specialized in one or two them. I could have explained the philosophical basis for them, some contemporary applications of them, or the history of them, in Greek philosophy and in the Bible; or I could have justified their objectivity, refuting modern subjectivist theories of them; or I could have talked about their generic definition: What is a value? But instead, I want to talk about the unity of them.

There are twelve of them. Is their unity merely generic, in that they are all values or virtues, as George Bush, Michael Gorbachev, George Steinbrenner, Paris Hilton, and Queen Elizabeth are all humans, or as 2, 3, and 4 are all numbers? Or do they have an organic unity, as the human body does? The human body has many subatomic particles unified into atoms, atoms unified into molecules, molecules unified into cells, cells unified into tissues, tissues unified into organs, and organs unified into systems: the circulatory system, the reproductive system, the digestive system, etc. What makes all these systems one? What makes them systems of one body? The answer was very clear and obvious to anyone with a philosophical education until quite recently. The answer is the soul.

Souls are not ghosts, and bodies are not machines. The

soul is the life of the body. That is its first function, which it shares with plants. Its second function, which it shares with animals, is twofold: awareness of the world through sense experience and the power to move the body to things desired such as food and sex, light, and water, things that give pleasure. Its third function is distinctively human: rational thinking and moral choosing. That is why we call it a rational soul. Animals have souls but not rational souls. Animals are conscious but not self-conscious. They are conscious of the world but not of themselves as subjects. They cannot say "I", which is the image of God, whose name is "I AM."

The point of this elementary philosophy lesson is that we have one soul, not three, so that the soul we call rational and free is also the life of the body. That is what makes the human body sacred, unlike the body of an animal. In saying that the soul is the life of the body, I mean something very simple: it unites all the bodily functions, systems, organs, tissues, molecules, and atoms. When the soul leaves the body, at death, these bodily functions cease, the systems cease to work, the organs cease to function, the tissues fall apart. The soul is the *unity* of the body, the one life of all the parts of the body.

This is an analogy for my question today: What is the unity, what is the soul, what is the life, of the twelve core values that Lumen has identified? It is the same as the soul of *all* values, including all lesser values. It is that which unifies the four cardinal virtues of Plato and Aristotle, which are the first four of Lumen's twelve core values. But Plato and Aristotle did not know the soul of all virtue, the soul of all values, the unity that holds them together and makes them function as one, as organs of the soul, or systems of the soul, so that virtue can be to the soul what health is to the body and make all the systems work together.

I want to tell you something very very simple today, something every one of you should know very clearly. I want to tell you just one point. I want to identify the soul, the life, the living, functional unity of all virtues and all values.

I hope you know the answer to that question because most people today do not. And that is the main reason why most people do not know the value of values, the virtue of virtues, or the goodness of goodness and the badness of badness anymore. According to a study by the Higher Education Research Institute, the percentage of Americans who thought getting rich was very important rose from 42 percent in 1967 to 75 percent in 2005, while the percentage who thought "developing a meaningful philosophy of life" was very important fell from 85 percent to 46 percent.[1]

According to a George Barna poll, "Americans are very comfortable with religious faith. Most adults and even teenagers see themselves as people of faith. . . . But their faith is rarely the focal point of their life or a critical factor in their decision-making." According to his poll, only 15 percent *of regular churchgoers*, who themselves make up only about 50 percent of Americans, give their relation to God as their first priority, and only 35 percent of regular churchgoers believe that God expects people to be holy.[2]

You see, we are modern, enlightened people. We are not primitive or barbarian. We have progressed. We are civilized. The following incident would never occur in modern America or Europe.

Turn the clock back to a primitive and terrible time, a time of vicious persecution against Christians by the Roman Empire, a time when only a small percentage of citizens were Christians, but all of them knew it might well cost them their life. One of the Church Fathers tells the story of

[1] *Catholic World Report*, April 2007.
[2] Ibid.

a Christian who refused to recant his faith and worship the emperor; he was executed at swordpoint and, as he died, wrote with his own blood in the sand: "Credo in unum Deum."

What is the difference between then and now? Then, every Christian knew one salient fact about Christianity: that it is either everything or nothing, either the world's stupidest lie or the world's ultimate truth; that if Jesus Christ is not literally everything to you, then He is nothing at all. Now, almost no one knows that anymore, and those who do, and say so, are labeled "fanatics".

I want to defend one fanaticism. Not fanaticism as such, not any other fanaticisms, but only one fanaticism: a fanaticism for Christ and His Lordship and His will as the one and only thing that matters in your life.

The answer to my question—what is the living soul and unity of all values—is Jesus Christ. That is why these twelve core values are valuable. Christ is not valuable because He is the teacher of these values or the incarnation of these values; rather, these values are valuable because they are the life of Christ. There are many values, but only one Lord. There are many colors into which His light divides when it passes through the prism of human life. But they are all colors of one light. There are many things that are useful and good and necessary relative to other things, but (according to Jesus Himself) there is *only one thing* that is absolutely necessary. That's what Jesus said to Martha. Poor Martha, though she was a good woman, full of faith and hope and love and good works, did not know that. And therefore she was unhappy and worried. Wise Mary did know that one thing, and therefore she was not unhappy or worried. That one thing was Jesus Christ Himself.

So instead of talking about twelve core values, I want to talk about the one that justifies them all. If these values were not the will of Christ for us, they would be worthless. If they were not the road by which we obey Him and love Him and please Him and travel to Him on this highway that is called time and life and lifetime, then they would be worthless. So I want to make just one point today, not twelve, and not even three. The only three-point sermon I will preach is this: first, I will tell you what I'm going to say, then I will say it, and then I will tell you what I said. But it will be the same single thing. Because seeing and living the single center is more important, is infinitely more important, than knowing and living all the other things. If there is no axle at the center of the wheel, then the spokes do not meet, and no matter how good and how many they are, the wheel does not hold together and does not move the vehicle that is your life down the road of time to the goal of God and union with God and eternal happiness with God. Those who enter Purgatory either do not know this, do not fully believe it, do not fully understand it, or do not fully live it; those who graduate from Purgatory all do. So I want to help you shorten your Purgatory.

But first, I want to justify this simplicity by briefly showing that all twelve of your core values are about this one thing, according to your own Handbook.

The first four values are character values or personal virtues. They are what the ancients called the Four Cardinal Virtues.

The first character value, practical wisdom or prudence, means, in the words of your Handbook, "Always know where you're going. Lacking a worthwhile destination or goal is today's most common imprudence. The flourishing self-help industry thrives on techniques but neglects purpose." Christ is our goal. Christ is our purpose. Christ is where we are going—unless Hell is where we are going.

The second character value, perseverance or fortitude, is

also for Christ because it is He who says "No one who puts his hand to the plow and looks back is fit for the kingdom of God" (Lk 9:62). The first virtue, knowing your end, necessitates the second, never giving up on the means. Christ is the only worthy object of Churchill's great advice, "Never, never, never, never . . . give in."

The third character value, fairness or justice, means Treat All Persons as They Deserve, that is, as what they are, that is, as created in the image of God, that is, as Christ says: "As you did it to one of the least of these my brethren, you did it to me" (Mt 25:40). We are to be fair to others because they are Christ's brethren; we are to be fair to them because of Christ, because we should treat them as we would treat Christ. More, we treat them *as* Christ in disguise.

The fourth character value, self-mastery, self-control, or temperance, means to master the Pleasure Principle, the selfish passion for selfish pleasure. St. Thomas Aquinas tells us that the only way to master a strong passion is by a stronger passion. The only passion stronger than the passion for self is the passion for Christ, for only Christ is greater than the self and yet the lover and savior of the self.

The next four values are faith values or religious values.

The fifth value, which the Handbook calls "spiritual drive", to quote its words, means "Decide what you want . . . thus, we want to have a nice house and a good job and plenty of money, but we never think about *why* we want those things." Christ is why we want what we want. If we do not want them because He wants them, we should not want them. "Thy will be done" is the very essence of true religion.

The sixth value, prayer, means simply practicing God's presence; and only Christ brings God to us and us to God. It is Christ who sits, walks, and stands beside us all day, and prayer is essentially the continual turning to Him who is really there.

The seventh value, stewardship, means using your world and your life for His Kingdom, having that as what the Handbook calls "your first priority around which all your other dreams and hopes and decisions gather like iron filings around a magnet"; knowing that "there is only one path: study Christ, love Christ, imitate Christ, follow Christ."

The eighth value, trust or confidence in God, absolutely depends on Christ, for it is Christ who shows us how much God is trustable because He shows us how much God loves us, on Calvary: *that* much. That is the object of our confidence. The Crucifix is the justification for the most wonderful and astonishing verse in the Bible, Romans 8:28; *that* is why we can be certain that "in everything God works for good with those who love him, who are called according to his purpose."

The last four values are "leadership values".

The ninth value, excellence in all things, is Christocentric because Christ is the one whose kingdom we are building with every stroke of our pen, our needle, or our sword.

The tenth value, integrity, or honesty, is ultimately to stand in the light, to endure the Heavenly light of Christ that His disciples saw on the Mount of Transfiguration. As your Handbook states, "Christ is your criterion for integrity."

The eleventh value, magnanimity, generosity, or active charity, is Christ's own commandment and the very nature of God. The ultimate reason for giving yourself to others is that that is the nature of ultimate reality. Each Person of the Trinity eternally gives Himself to the other two in endless and infinite joy. The essential reason we are here on earth is to train for our participation in that destiny.

The twelfth value, influence, is simply the courage and

passion in spreading of the other eleven, that is, of Christ's Kingdom, in everything we do.

So these twelve values are simply an unpacking of what St. Paul meant when he said, "For to me to live is Christ" (Phil 1:21). The meaning of life is one word. It is His name.

The earliest of all Christian creeds, mentioned twice in the New Testament, in Paul's letters, is also the most basic and the shortest. It consists of just three words: Jesus is Lord.

Muslims pray five times a day, because of the need to overcome *ghaflah*, which means our innate forgetfulness, with *dhikr*, which means remembering. We must outdo them. We should pray this simple three-word creed fifty times a day.

That word "Lord" means two things. First, it means that Jesus is God. The word *Kyrios* is never used in the Bible for any human lord. So it means adoration. Second, it means obedience, for it means that since Jesus is God He demands to be your God, your Lord, your everything, and that the single most important thing you can possibly do in your life is to surrender your whole life to Him. In other words, the meaning of life is to become a saint.

A French Catholic writer of a century ago, Léon Bloy, frequently wrote this sentence. It is one of the most profound sentences I have ever read: "There is only one tragedy, in the end: not to have been a saint."

That is the meaning of life. The meaning of life is to be a saint. Nothing less. God is not satisfied with anything less. He is "easy to please but hard to satisfy". Jesus tells us we must "be perfect, as your heavenly Father is perfect" (Mt 5:48). That sounds to us outrageously high. We don't want to accept that. But how dare we correct the Creator and Designer of human life concerning the purpose of human life?

All right, then, so the end is sanctity. What is the means to the end? Sanctity comes only by struggle, "inner struggle", *jihad*. All the Christian saints strongly agree with the Koran there. There is not a single exception. They all describe the Christian life as an *agon*, a Greek word that means "effort" or "work". It is the root of the word "agony". One of the Desert Fathers, Abbot Agathon, said, "prayer is warfare to the last breath."

There are many wars that can be avoided by good diplomacy. But not this war. For this war is not a part of life; this war is life itself.

There are many enemies that can be negotiated with. But not this enemy. For this enemy is not flesh and blood but principalities and powers, evil spirits, fallen angels (unless Jesus and the saints are all fools or liars). This enemy is not merely some evil men or some evil things but evil itself.

There are many causes that are worth large investments of our devotion, time, and energy. But not this cause. This cause demands all. For it is not some good things or some good men but goodness itself.

Not everyone is a career soldier. There are many enlistments that are not for life. But not this enlistment. For this enlistment is not only for life but for eternity.

There are many armies who lose not only battles but wars. But not this army. For this army is God's army, and its front lines are composed of angels and chariots of fire.

There are many commanding officers who sometimes make mistakes in battle plans. But not this commanding officer. For He alone is God, and He alone is infallible. Whenever there is a conflict between His marching orders and the ones we invent, ours are always proved to be wrong and His right in the end.

There are many defeats that leave a remnant of people

and of hope. But not defeat in this war. For defeat in this war means, not a strategic retreat so as to fight again some other day, but entering the prisoner-of-war camp that has no exit and over whose door hangs Dante's sign, "Abandon all hope, ye who enter here."

There are many victories that are tainted, for they were achieved by means that were not wholly good, by unrighteous weapons. But not this victory. For it is achieved only by the weapons of righteousness. You cannot fight for Christ with Satan's weapons.

There are many victories for peace that last only until the next outbreak of war. But not this peace. For it is the peace of eternity, which lasts forever.

There are many conflicts that can be settled by compromise. For life is full of grays, rather than absolute blacks and whites. But not this conflict. It is total, absolute, and eternal, for it is the conflict between black and white, evil and good. All grays are mixtures of this black and this white.

There are many goals that are optional for a man to choose. But not this goal. For the goal of this war is the goal of life itself.

There are many defeats that are not final. But not this defeat. For it is final, eternal death, the "second death", from which there is no resurrection. It is life's only final tragedy.

There are many rewards that are not complete. After we receive them, we move on to other, better things. But not this reward. For it is the infinite, unimaginable, unending ecstasy of bliss and light in entering God's own spiritual bridal chamber, entering an eternal and indissoluble marriage to God Himself.

There are many investments that demand less than all our resources, for if they fail we will still have something left for tomorrow and for others. But not this investment. For if we lose this, we have nothing left at all for any tomorrow at all.

There are many wars that cost too much. But this one does not cost too much, even though it costs everything. T. S. Eliot defines being a Christian in these words: "A condition of complete simplicity / (Costing not less than everything)".

The meaning of life is to be a saint. But what is a saint? A saint is a totally single-minded person. Kierkegaard wrote a book with the great title: *Purity of Heart Is to Will One Thing*. That is the definition of a saint. It is Jesus' definition, too. Here is His first and greatest commandment: "Love the Lord your God with *all* your heart, and with all your soul, and with all your mind, and with all your strength" (Mk 12:30). Jesus never exaggerated.

"All", "total", "absolute", "only". These are words the world calls "fanatical". You cannot be a saint without deeply disturbing the world, because you cannot be a saint without being a fanatic.

Ancient Rome did not persecute any other religions except for Judaism and Christianity. They were very tolerant. You were allowed to worship any god you wished. But the claim that there was only one God, that this God demanded total service from everyone, was so intolerant that tolerance responded by torture and mass murder. The claim that Christ will not share His lordship with other gods was unendurable. It was a war to the death. Christians did not offer Christ as one of many ways to salvation. For Christ did not offer himself thus, and Christians were fanatically loyal and faithful to His holy fanaticism. They would not be more tolerant and broad-minded than Christ. Oh, they often said that Christ had followers outside the Church, too— Socrates, for instance, and perhaps many, many others (Jesus

Himself had refused to satisfy His disciples' curiosity about comparative population statistics of Heaven and Hell); and many who bore the name of Christian, or even apostle, like Judas, were enemies of Christ. But this was the nonnegotiable scandal: that "there is no other name under heaven given among men by which we must be saved" (Acts 4:12). Jesus said, "I am the way, and the truth, and the life, no one comes to the Father, but by me" (Jn 14:6), and Christians refused to correct Christ on this or any other matter.

"Fanatic" is our civilization's new F-word. There is literally no label more losing, no insult more insulting, no dismissal more dismissive, than that. At a fashionable cocktail party, if you confess that you are a nuclear terrorist or a foreign spy or that you have invented a new way to commit suicide or that you practice sex with crocodiles, you will attract a buzzing crowd of human flies and probably a big book contract. But if you confess that Jesus is your Lord, you will feel the temperature suddenly drop, and you will find yourself alone.

Why must we be fanatics? Because the fundamental principle of all morality is the 3-R principle, Right Response to Reality. Be real. Let life mirror truth. Live in reality, not in fantasy. Let your subjective reality conform to objective reality. And the ultimate truth of objective reality is Christ, for Christ is God, and God is the prime reality, the first reality, the greatest reality, the Creator of all other reality, the standard of reality for everything else. That is why you must love God with all your heart, soul, mind, and strength. And that is why that is the first and greatest commandment. God deserves the same place in our hearts and in our lives, in the subjective reality that we are free to make, as He has in objective reality: namely, Alpha and Omega, first and last, beginning and end, of all.

And that is also why the second commandment is like unto it, love your neighbor as yourself: because of what your neighbor really is: God's image, God's kid, God's beloved. If your neighbor were only a bunch of cells that had evolved by chance in an unintelligent universe, the only reasons to love him would be subjective, would be *your* reasons. But since your neighbor is the King's kid, not King Kong's kid, he is to be loved as he is, and you are also to be loved as you are, that is, as God's kid. That is why all people have intrinsic value. No man, no government, no ideology, no philosophy, no human consensus can give man intrinsic value. And if they could, they could also take it away at will.

Our main enemy is sin, and the main sin is pride, egotism, playing God. That's why no human psychology or meditation technique or techniques of group interaction or critical thinking can touch life's greatest problem: our innate, voracious, consuming egotism. Our egotism is usually very cleverly and politely disguised. But the real truth is that I'm *not* OK, and neither are you. And you can't do a damned thing about it. But God can. Alcoholics Anonymous has it right about those two things. And so does the Bible: Point One: "Without Me you can do nothing"; Point Two: "with God all things are possible." We are more willing to believe the second truth, the good news, than the first, which is the bad news. But the bad news is the precondition for the good news. The bad news is that we can no more save ourselves than we can lift ourselves up by our own bootstraps. We are like infected physicians reinfecting ourselves in the very act of injecting ourselves with our own man-made medicines. Because the infection is sin, and this infection is not external to the self: it is the selfishness of the self itself. We must step out of ourselves, out of the control room of our starship, out of the master's suite and into the servants' quarters. The

Muslims have a lot of things wrong, but they have this most important of all things in life utterly right: the single most important thing in human life is "Islam", surrender, that is, surrender to God, because "there is no God but God."

And then, once we have surrendered to God, we will never, never, never surrender to God's enemies. We will far sooner die than do evil. The difference between life and death is trivial compared to the difference between good and evil, for that is the difference between God and Satan.

When God takes control, He is like the traffic cop at the busy city corner. He directs all the traffic aright, cars and pedestrians. Without Him, everyone goes where he wills, that is, in every possible different direction. There are chaos and collisions and crashes.

Men without God are like ships without rudders, subject to every shift of wind and tide, fads and fashions, pressures and influences, drifters.

Putting God second is like putting the top button of your coat into the second buttonhole. It throws off all the others. When the second button is put into the first hole, nothing comes out right. When subjective reality does not conform to objective reality, nothing comes out right. Sanctity is sanity.

The meaning of life is to become like the Mississippi River. All the other hundreds and thousands of little and medium-sized rivers flow into it, and it unifies them all and takes all their waters to the ocean. Physical gravity moves all matter to unity, especially heavy matter like water. There is a spiritual gravity, too, a God-gravity, and there is one and only one magnet pulling all that is good, and that is God. We must learn to be spiritual Mississippis.

When we sin, we are insane. We choose misery over joy. And we know it—we know that sin leads to misery, by repeated, consistent experience. We are not rational; we are addicts, sinaholics. The alcoholic knows very clearly that he is ruining his life and his happiness, and he does it anyway. So does the sinaholic. This is how insane we are: Here is a choice. On this side, joy. On that side, misery. Now which will you choose? Uh, let's see now, I'm not quite sure. . . . That is insanity. We are spiritually insane. That is what Original Sin means.

God is a jealous God because there is only one of Him. He will not share His glory with another, because there is no other. And Jesus is God incarnate. If you do not believe that, you are simply not a Christian. And if you go to church on Sunday and speak the words of the Nicene Creed that say that, but you do not really believe it, then you are a hypocrite.

And therefore, since God will not share His glory with another and since Jesus is God, therefore Jesus will not share His glory with another. That Jesus is Lord is a very simple and very clear thought. It takes almost no time to say it and no complex meditation techniques. It is like a buck private looking up to see the face of the four-star general looking down at him. We should see Christ our commander always because He is present always, and we should spiritually salute Him fifty times a day until love and obedience become one.

We feel more comfortable putting Christ in a bottle, like a genie or medicine, and using Him only when we feel it's necessary. If our prayers honestly spoke our hearts, they would say something like this: "Lord, please bless me a bit over here and over there. Please tidy up the parts of my life that I do not like. But nothing more, please. That will do for now. Thank you very much. You are dismissed. You may go now."

There is only one way to avoid this insanity, which stands

in the way of our being saints, stands in the way of our attaining the meaning of our lives. And that way is what the world calls fanaticism and what Muslims call "surrender" and what Jesus calls obeying the first and greatest commandment.

Jesus said to Martha: "One thing is needful" (Lk 10:42). Only one thing! This is a statement of total fanaticism, total narrow-mindedness. And what is that one thing? Jesus Himself. And He is exactly the opposite of narrow. "My God will supply every need of yours according to his riches in glory in Christ Jesus" (Phil 4:19).

There are only two ways to live, and both have an absolute. Christ's way is to let God be God, to acknowledge the real absolute. Our alternatives, our idolatries, diverse as they are, always amount to the same thing: choosing ourselves instead of God as the absolute. For whether we serve abstract idols like capitalism, communism, Americanism, pacifism, terrorism, theism, atheism, or any other ism, or whether we serve concrete idols like money, sex, fame, power, and comfort or self-esteem and peace of mind, in all cases, we are choosing them on our own authority and for ourselves. If we try to be broad-minded and scatter our loves over this world of many good things, we will find that we are really very narrow-minded, for the ego is a very, very narrow thing. But if we accept Christ's narrow way and have the mind of Christ, if we live the narrow-minded life of Christ-mindedness, we will find that we are as broad as God. Let the ego die, pass through the needle's eye, and your soul will soar and fly through the sky. But if, instead, you try with your own wings to fly, you'll fall into your own I.

Joshua, whose name means exactly the same as Jesus, said to Israel: "Choose this day whom you will serve . . . but as for me and my house, we will serve the LORD" (Josh 24:15).

Fifteen hundred years later, Jesus said, "No one can serve two masters" (Mt 6:24). C. S. Lewis put it this way: "There are only two kinds of people in the end: those who say to God, 'Thy will be done', and those to whom God says, in the end, '*Thy* will be done'" (emphasis added).

Jesus came to establish the kingdom of God. What is the kingdom of God? "The kingdom of God is in your midst", said Jesus (Lk 17:21). It is not in the world. It is in the heart. The kingdom of God is the total reign of God over the human heart. The kingdom of God is sanctity.

A saint is not perfect. A saint is a sinner. A saint goes to confession frequently. David was a saint. God called him "a man after my heart" (Acts 13:22), not because he never sinned, but because he never worshipped other gods, as most of the other kings of Israel did. His heart was wholly given to God. He was a whole man. He was a fanatic.

And if, and only if, you are like David in being a fanatic, you can be like David in being a powerful leader and instrument for God's work in this world. The fulfillment of all the goals of the Lumen Institute begins here. If there was the slightest doubt of that in the mind of a single one of you here today, even though all the rest of you were bored with this talk because you knew all this with total clarity, this talk was necessary.

8

Traditionalism and Progressivism

I'm often asked whether I'm a liberal or a conservative. Once, when I answered that I was apolitical, they asked me, "But are you an apolitical liberal or an apolitical conservative?"

That's the logic of the story of the man who was walking alone down a dark street in Belfast during the Troubles, and he suddenly felt a strong arm pinning his hands and a knife at his throat, and a voice that demanded, "Are ye a Catlick or are ye a Protestant?" He thought: "I have only a 50 percent chance of survival if I guess." So he said, "I'm an atheist, thank God." The knife did not move. The voice demanded, "A Catlick atheist or a Protestant atheist?"

The other answer I give to the question whether I classify myself as a liberal or a conservative is that I used to classify myself as a liberal and vote for Democrats (while holding my nose). Now I classify myself as a conservative and vote for Republicans (also while holding my nose). But I haven't changed my mind on any of the issues; they just changed the labels.

Time changes political labels so much that they are always misleading and sometimes simply meaningless. So does place. Liberalism in Europe is very different from liberalism in America. For instance, conservatism in Europe tends to be pro-government and liberalism more libertarian, while in America it is the reverse.

But if conservatism simply means wanting to conserve the status quo, whatever it is, and if liberalism means wanting to change it, then we may as well use the words "traditionalism" and "progressivism" because they do not carry any ideological implications, they just talk about change. That's what was in Ambrose Bierce's mind when he gave these definitions of a liberal and a conservative in *The Devil's Dictionary*: "[The conservative is] a statesman who is enamored of existing evils, as distinguished from the liberal, who wishes to replace them with others."

Since conservatives, by definition, are happy with what they have and want to conserve it, while liberals are unhappy with what they have and want to change it, conservatives are therefore by definition happier than liberals. For instance, women are usually liberal, or progressive, and men conservative about where the furniture should go, while men are usually liberal, or progressive, and women conservative about where the soldiers should go. Men want the furniture to stay home, and women want the soldiers to stay home.

This can get confusing. So it's better that I write about progressivism and traditionalism rather than liberalism and conservatism. Better yet, my question is not just these two isms in the abstract but in relation to Christianity: Is Christianity a form of traditionalism or a form of progressivism?

My answer, to put the bottom line at the top, is the same as the answer the Scotsman gave when he heard an Englishman and an American arguing about whether the word is pronounced "Neether" or "nighther". He said, "It's nayther." Christianity considered, traditionalism and progressivism are both heresies.

There will be two parts to this essay. (I say "will be" because I haven't begun it yet; I've just softened you up by telling a couple of silly jokes.) The two parts will be:

principles and practice, or philosophical-theological points and cultural-sociological points. First, I will explain the source of both heresies, and then I will try to apply the Christian orthodoxy that is the alternative to these two heresies to the desperate problem of our day, which is the embarrassingly obvious fact that our culture is diving deeper and deeper into desperately dumb decadence with a deep desire for death and damnation.

Meanwhile, have a nice day.

Traditionalism and progressivism are both heresies, and they come from the same source, even though they are opposites. In fact, it is *because* they come from the same source that they come in the form of opposites. In dogma as in morality, errors usually come in opposite pairs, as old Aristotle taught us. Cowardice and rashness, prodigality and stinginess, wrath and insensitivity, ambition and sloth, shyness and buffoonery, shamelessness and shamefacedness, presumption and despair are all opposite vices, because "there are an infinity of angles at which one falls, only one at which one stands." That's from Chesterton, our modern Aristotle, our modern apostle of common sense.

In theology, we find the denial of Christ's humanity in docetism and of His divinity in Arianism; we find the denial of free will in Calvinism and of predestination in Arminianism; we find the denial of God's Threeness in Unitarianism and of His oneness in polytheism; we find the denial of images in iconoclasm and the worship of them in superstition; we find the denial of human materiality in gnosticism and all forms of spiritualism and the denial of human spirituality in materialism.

(The modern form of gnosticism, by the way, often coexists with materialism in both denying and idolizing physical sexuality, viewing the human body as a mere neutral object for manipulation and in idolizing any manipulation of it that causes sexual pleasure.)

In each case, the great truth that is denied in opposite ways is paradoxical. A paradox is an apparent contradiction but not a real one. Thus the great truths of the faith are always a scandal to modern reason, which is calculating and manipulative and technological and utilitarian. But the great truths are a source of wisdom and joy to premodern reason; which is contemplative and receptive, wondering and humble.

The usual source of the heretic's error is the use of modern reason rather than premodern reason; reason that crawls along a horizontal line like a worm rather than rising into the light like a butterfly or like the dew that came down from Heaven and returns there invisibly by evaporation. (Evaporation is an icon of the great mystery of life through death, the fulfillment of the self by the death of the self.)

In the case of the twin heresies of traditionalism and progressivism, the source of both errors is thinking of human history and culture merely horizontally rather than vertically, temporally rather than eternally, naturally rather than supernaturally. The worm crawling across the ground either returns to where he was in the past or moves to progress to a new ground in the future. He seeks, as his goal, either a return to a certain temporal state in the past that he idolatrously worships as his ideal or a moving away from it to an opposite state in the idealized future, which again he idolizes. The god of both the traditionalist and the progressivist is a god in time. He, she, or it has no eternity. The god of both progressivism and traditionalism is temporal rather than eternal.

Many people simply cannot understand the concept of eternity. Eternity does not mean endless time or even infinite time. That is just progressivism in disguise. Eternity means another dimension entirely, a timeless dimension, a vertical dimension, an absolute that judges all horizontal movements in time, both traditionalist and progressivist, by its own standard. For its standard is the true God.

Thus, Alexander Solzhenitsyn was exactly on target when, in his great Templeton Address of 1983, one of the greatest and most prophetic speeches in the history of Western civilization, when he diagnosed the ultimate cause of all the ills and decadences and self-destructivenesses of our culture of death in one simple sentence: "Men have forgotten God." The sophisticates and intellectuals and chattering classes that heard that speech were outraged. They never forgave him. People will forgive you for being wrong, but they will never forgive you for being right.

Christian orthodoxy is not traditionalism any more than it is progressivism. Orthodoxy worships the God of eternity Who is always met in the present, which is the only moment of time in which any of us can live and Who both revealed Himself in a definitive way in our past and gave us a hope and a task to be perfected in our future. But our past and our future are not God's past and God's future. God is much too real to have a dead past or an unborn future.

The eternal God revealed Himself to us in our past, and this divine revelation in the past is definitive because God is eternal. When Truth enters history, Truth changes history; history does not change Truth. When Christ was baptized by John the Baptist in the waters of the Jordan, He sanctified the waters of baptism rather than being sanctified by them. Similarly, Christ was not made or made new by anything, but He made all things new because He came, not from the past or the future, but from eternity. That is why the

Church is absolute about divinely revealed dogma; it cannot change; only our unpacking of it, our understanding of it, can change.

God's mission for His Church is to march into the future armed with the wisdom of the past. Secular movements sometimes do this, too, but Christianity is different because our foundation is not the past but the eternal truth God revealed and incarnated in the past, and our goal is not merely a better world in the future but a world beyond time, a world beyond the world.

In the words of the Letter to the Hebrews, we are not children of past time or of future time but are "strangers and exiles on the earth" (that is, in time). We are not traditionalists because, as Hebrews goes on to say, "people who speak thus make it clear that they are seeking a homeland. If they had been thinking of that land from which they had gone out, they would have had opportunity to return. But as it is, they desire a better country, that is, a heavenly one" (Heb 11:13–16). Heaven is not in future time any more than it is in past time; it is in eternity. It is not in this universe, in which time and space, matter and energy, are relative to each other.

In Christ's day, the Pharisees were traditionalists. That is why they were scandalized by Christ, who said, "Behold, I make all things new." The Sadducees, on the other hand, were the progressivists, the modernists, the worshippers of their culture's version of the modern scientific enlightenment, who denied the miraculous and the supernatural. Christ always alienated opposites. He also alienated both Herodian collaborationists and Zealot rebels. Chesterton describes Him this way in his wonderfully unorthodox masterpiece *Orthodoxy*. He says:

Suppose we heard an unknown man spoken of by many men. Suppose we were puzzled to hear that some men said he was too tall and some too short; some objected to his fatness, some lamented his leanness; some thought him too dark, and some too fair. One explanation (as has been already admitted) would be that he might be an odd shape. But there is another explanation. He might be the right shape. Outrageously tall men might feel him to be short. Very short men might feel him to be tall. Old bucks who are growing stout might consider him insufficiently filled out; old beaux who were growing thin might feel that he expanded beyond the narrow lines of elegance.[1]

Thus, Christians are criticized for being too pacifistic and too militaristic, too feminine (most churchgoers are women) and too masculine ("male chauvinism"), too absolutistic about justice (hard-hearted) and too absolutistic about mercy (too soft-hearted). In fact, they are at war with war, in love with love, and absolutistic about all absolutes, including both justice and mercy. They are at war with greed, lust, and pride, with the world, the flesh, and the Devil, and therefore they make peace with neighbor, self, and God rather than with the world, the flesh and the Devil, and they practice poverty, chastity, and obedience rather than greed, lust, and pride.

In Christ's day, the traditionalists were in the majority (though there was also a minority of progressivists who criticized Him for being insufficiently up to date). Today it is the progressivists who are in charge. Thus, the Church is criticized for being too traditional (though there is also

---

[1] G. K. Chesterton, *Orthodoxy*, in *Collected Works*, vol. 1 (San Francisco: Ignatius Press, 1986), 294–95.

a minority of traditionalists who criticize her for being too progressive, too open to the uncertain future).

How, then, do we confront our modern culture with these principles? How do we give life to a culture of death? How do we practice the new evangelization?

We must first diagnose the disease before we can cure it.

Solzhenitsyn's diagnosis is the true one—we have forgotten God—but what new forms has this forgetfulness taken in our culture? We are idolaters, of course—all sins are forms of idolatry, that is why the first commandment is first—but idols come in many forms. What do the monsters look like today? Let us X-ray our disease.

Darwin, Marx, and Freud are probably the three most influential modern thinkers. They are all atheists, materialists, naturalists, and immoralists. They all give us excuses for exculpation. We act badly, not by free will and sin, but because we are determined by evolution, (we are all apes with computers), or, because we are determined by history (we are chained capitalists), or, because we are determined by our id (we are all sex addicts).

If we want to find the key to understanding Marxism and why it has exercised such a magnetic attraction on our intellectuals, we need to look at Nietzsche rather than Marx. It is the will to power that fascinates intellectuals, because intellectuals are usually physically weaker than ordinary people and need to compensate or cover this up. Communism offers power   power over capitalist "haves", power over the future, power over money, power over things, power over the world. Marxism is technologism applied to human historical reality. It is Bacon's "conquest of nature" applied to human nature.

Freud is much easier to understand. Like the utilitarians,

Freud is a hedonist. His appeal is not so much power as pleasure, and pleasure is reduced to sexual pleasure because Freudians and utilitarians have astonishingly shallow imaginations.

Darwin provides the pseudo-scientific justification for both reductionisms by denying the eternal soul and reducing us to the material causes out of which we evolved. That's why our culture can never question Darwin, even though it can question Marx and Freud.

I call this pseudo-science, by the way, not only because of the strictly scientific holes in the theory of evolution, which may some day be plugged up by future science, but because universal evolutionism is not science at all but ideology and philosophy and even theology in disguise. It is reductionism: we are merely our material cause, with no first efficient cause, no Creator; and no formal cause, no Designer of our identity; and no final cause, no natural ends or purposes to human nature. That is the common assumption of scientism.

Of course scientism is self-contradictory, since there is no possible proof by science itself of the assumption that science is the only road to certainty. The scientific method cannot prove that all legitimate proof must be by the scientific method. But this is merely common sense and, therefore, a scandal to intellectuals. As we say in academia, there are some ideas that are so illogical that only a Ph.D. could possibly believe them.

Our culture's god is not science as such, however, but its application, technology. Francis Bacon prophesied this new *summum bonum*, "man's conquest of nature", five centuries ago. As C. S. Lewis pointed out in *The Abolition of Man*, technology and magic arose together, in the Renaissance, because they share this same Baconian end, the conquest of nature. Here is one of the most illuminating sentences I have ever read about our culture: "For the wise men of old, the cardinal problem had been how to conform the soul to reality, and the solution had been knowledge, self-discipline, and virtue. For magic and applied science alike the problem is to subdue reality to the wishes of men: the solution is a technique [that is, technology]." Pure science and pure religion seek to conform the soul to truth, to reality—science to the reality of nature and religion to the reality of supernature. Technology and magic both seek power, technology by natural means and magic by supernatural means.

Of course technology itself is innocent. It is the worship of it, the idolization of it, that is evil. Adam tilling the garden was technology. Noah's ark was technology. Solomon's temple and Notre Dame Cathedral were technology. So was Cain's rock and the Roman art of crucifixion and the gas chambers in Auschwitz and the bombs at Hiroshima and Nagasaki.

There are many prescriptions for social happiness that do not work. Traditionalism and progressivism are two of them.

What will work? Saints and sages.

Perhaps enough saints and sages can arise to be a critical mass to transform our whole culture. It does not look as if this is likely. Despite the two greatest saints of the twentieth century, John Paul II and Mother Teresa, our culture is accelerating into a *Brave New World* (which is a miraculously prophetic book: no one who cares about our culture's future can afford not to read it). Only fifty years ago, no one believed we would have abortion on demand, the hookup culture, gay marriage, and euthanasia. What used to be crimes are now celebrated. What's next? Group marriages, bestiality, incest, pedophilia, and cannibalism? Why not, if it's consensual? The basic ethical rule of the subjectivistic utilitarianism of our culture is that the autonomy and free choice of the individual is totally unrestricted except by that of other individuals. There is no longer any such thing as human nature, the human essence, or natural human ends, goals, and purposes. There is only the will to power and the demand for pleasure.

Humanae Vitae was prophetic in seeing the issue of contraception as only the first of the consequences of abandoning the idea of natural law and natural ends, an idea that was assumed in all premodern moralities in all cultures. The fundamental principle has changed. There is no longer any objective law, either natural or supernatural, no longer any human nature or natural ends, but only individual will, freedom, and autonomy. The logic is inexorable. If abortion, why not infanticide? I once convinced some very intelligent pro-choice feminists that there was no possible argument that justified abortion that did not also justify infanticide. They thought about it seriously for a while and their response, the next day, was, quite seriously, to tell me that my arguments had convinced them. They had changed their minds. "Good for you", I said. "So you're pro-life now?" No, they said, they were pro-infanticide.

And once you can kill inconvenient infants, why not inconvenient teenagers? If the human will and human law are what gives personhood, only sentiment, not reason, stands in the way of whatever genocide you want. Our present sentiments are compassionate to Jews, Blacks, women, and homosexuals. It is not so compassionate to Down Syndrome babies, over 90 percent of whom are now murdered before they can pollute their parents' perfect plans. For the first time in American history, religious conscience is being ignored and coerced by government policies. In Canada, it is illegal, it is "hate speech", to express biblical opinions about homosexuality. How likely is it that this will be the only such issue?

Unlike natural law, human sentiments, feelings, and opinions are notoriously flexible and manipulable by media. Once, in some places in our culture, human sentiments were toxic to Jews, Blacks, gays, and others. Nothing but sentiment and will prevent this from happening again, because there is no substantive answer to the question *Why not* do this or that thing that I very much want to do?

All other answers to that question *why not*? have already been swept away in principle by our moral relativism. The only remaining obstacles are more of the same weak and sentimental and merely traditional and temporary scruples or—or something unchanging. Something like God.

But there *is* nothing like God. "Who is like God?" is the literal meaning of the name "Michael". As the Muslims rightly repeat, "Only God is God." Islam has half of God: His will, His justice, His righteousness. Christianity has also the other half of God: His love. But when a strong Islam with its strong half-God confronts a weak Christianity with a weak whole-God, the strong half-God will displace the weak whole-God in the culture, because even though it is not truer, it is stronger. It is willing to suffer. We are not. When a Cross without Christ confronts a Christ without a Cross, the Cross will win. That is why Islam is winning the West today. Thank God, it is not winning Africa or Asia or Latin America. God is preparing a new Christian culture in the global South to replace the dying one in the North. He has done that sort of thing a number of times before. He never promised us that the gates of Hell would not prevail against America or the West or anything else except His Church.

In the West, we are relentlessly forgetting or denying God

more and more. Religion is in continuing and accelerating decline in every part of Western civilization. The two largest religious groups in America are ex-Catholics and cafeteria Catholics. What can we do to reverse our failure and achieve success in fulfilling the Great Commission?

I take my first answer from Mother Teresa's most quoted saying: God did not put me on this earth to be successful, He put me here to be faithful. We are asking the wrong question!

I take my second answer from Pope Emeritus Benedict. It has been called "the Benedict option". Cardinal Ratzinger took the name Benedict because he saw his task, and the Church's task, in present time as the preservation of monastic islands of sanity in a world gone insane so that when that world died, the truth would still be alive for a future social resurrection. What the physical monks did in the Dark Ages to secular civilization, spiritual monks must do in these darker Dark Ages to sacred civilization.

Saint Thomas More is a model for us here. He was not a monk physically, but he was interiorly. He lived in a world as wicked and as dangerous as ours, and he survived, his soul survived even though his body was martyred, and became part of the glorious and unstoppable blood that is the seed of the Church. He survived because he was not a traditionalist or a progressivist but "a man for all seasons" because his God was not a God *of* or *from* any season of time but *for* all seasons because *from* eternity. (By the way, I vote for *A Man for All Seasons*, starring Paul Scofield, as the greatest movie ever made and certainly the one that answers our present need the most powerfully.)

Will this work? In the long run, yes, necessarily, not only because God holds the ultimate strings of power but also because the human heart was not designed in Harvard or in

Hollywood but in Heaven. The gates of Hell cannot prevail over the Church that is holy, the Church that produces the only truly happy people in the world, the saints.

Persecution cannot stop the saints. We need not fear persecution. Jesus explicitly told us that: fear not him who can only kill the body; fear him who can kill the soul, in Hell. The world's most efficient machine for persecution, the Roman Empire, only multiplied Christians by persecuting them. If Islam conquers the West and tries to kill Christianity by killing all Christians, they will only do the same thing. We need not fear our foreign Herods or our domestic Pilates or even our Judas Iscariots. For God used even Judas as an instrument for our redemption. We need fear only our own inner Herods and Pilates and Judases, our own sins and cowardice and betrayals. Yet even them God will overcome. The power of His mercy is infinitely greater than the power of our sins. If the Church survived the Borgia popes, she can survive even the pedophile priests and cowardly coverup bishops.

It may take half a millennium to get through our new Dark Age. It took half a millennium for a new civilization to emerge from the chrysalis of monasticism after the Dark Ages. And it may take a disaster, likely a nuclear war, after which saints will again convince the world of the truth of Christ's religion by practicing it heroically, as many did during the dying Roman Empire. They were the only people in the world who risked their lives ministering to the victims of plagues. You can ignore or refute any argument in words, but you can't ignore or refute that argument in deeds.

Let us pray that there is an easier way. We can do that because we do not know whether there is or not. We do not know the road to the apocalypse and the Parousia and the end of time; we do not know how long it is or how hard it is. But we do know, with certainty, its end and who will win.

Saints will win the world. But *only* saints will win the world. Nothing less will do for our culture, Not even the greatest prophets, sages, philosophers, theologians, psychologists, or politicians can save the world. If Moses, Socrates, Aristotle, Thomas Aquinas, Viktor Frankl, Abraham Lincoln, and Martin Luther King all came back to our culture, they could not save it, for it would dismiss them all as dead white European heterosexual conservative judgmental moralistic males.

But saints can save the world. If there had been ten righteous men in Sodom, they would have saved that world from the divine fire. Perhaps it would take only ten more righteous men to save San Francisco. Perhaps it would take only ten more Mother Teresas. There is one and only one reason why ten of us are not those next ten Mother Teresas: because we do not want to be.

Saints will save our world because there is a spiritual gravity as well as a physical gravity and a spiritual natural selection as well as a biological natural selection. No one can see God without falling in love with Him, and no one can meet a saint without meeting God in him or her. That is the good news: that in a world dedicated to the will to power, there is no power greater than that of sanctity; and that in a world dedicated to the pursuit of selfish pleasure, there is no pleasure greater than that of unselfish love of God and man. No one can ignore or refute the joy of a saint.

That's the good news. The bad news is that there is no other way because of the law of causality: the effect cannot exceed the cause. Nothing less than the highest thing can produce the second highest thing. That includes both all the things in the past and all the things in the future and, therefore, both traditionalism and progressivism.

Our age worships the future. We must not respond by worshipping the past. Our orthodoxy, though revealed in the past, comes not from past time but from eternity *through* the past, and it lights our road not just to future time but to eternity. True traditionalism loves the past only as Jews love their law and their prophets: it is not God but a communication link with God.

This true traditionalism is the true progressivism. Modern progressivism, and the idea of secular temporal progress, is already old. (It is also false: we are only smarter, not wiser, more powerful as a race but weaker as individuals, more sensitive but not holier, and more luxury-filled but not happier than our ancestors.) The old faith in progressivism has become the new orthodoxy. And when the old progressivism becomes the new orthodoxy, the only possible new and true progressivism is the old orthodoxy. When revolution becomes the tradition, traditionalism becomes the only remaining revolution.

9

C. S. Lewis, J. R. R. Tolkien, and the Culture Wars

What a strange title. What a questionable title. How dare I treat the beautiful writings of these two geniuses as if they were mere fodder, mere raw material for manipulation and misuse? They died over fifty years ago; can't I leave their dead bones undisturbed? They were Brits; how dare I ask them to speak to Americans about a problem—culture wars —whose very existence is admitted only by Americans, and only by conservative Americans to boot? Liberals, the aggressors in the culture wars, deny the very existence of culture wars, for the same reason the Nazis denied that they invaded Poland.

By the way, the fact that Europeans do not admit the culture war exists proves, more than anything else, that they have already lost it. The continent that used to be called Christendom is fast becoming a Muslim continent, and not by shedding blood in wars—we stopped that attempt at Poitiers and at Vienna and at Lepanto—but by shedding *menstrual* blood, that is, by a far harder, costlier, and nobler sacrifice than war: by having children. And I candidly have to say they deserve it, and we deserve to lose it.

But how dare we use two Brits to help us win it? We fought against them for our independence in 1776; are we now admitting our dependence on them and asking them to fight for us now? My answer is, as they say in Maine, *Ayup.*

Wordsworth wrote to the dead poet Milton: "Milton!

thou shouldst be living at this hour: / England hath need of thee: she is a fen" ("London 1802"). I say the same to Lewis and Tolkien. But more than just writing to them care of the Dead Poets Society, I call them up from their unquiet graves and demand they speak to us about our little war for the sake of the survival of that little local thing called Western civilization. I do this because, being a genuine first-class fool, I claim the right to rush in with my pen where angels fear to tread with their swords, for even if the pen is *not mightier* than the sword, it is more arrogant.

Tolkien first. *The Lord of the Rings* is us. Its story is our story, its battle is our battle, its world is our world, and its protagonists and antagonists are ours, too. We are fighting hordes of intellectual orcs, and we are an unlikely fellowship of assorted kinds of creatures, mainly hobbits. In fact, I will now identify the Nine Walkers. Since our battle is for the survival of the West, I will act as if I were in an old Western movie, and, like a Texas sheriff, I will give out nine badges to nine deputies.

I assign the role of Gandalf to Jim Patrick. He even looks like Gandalf. And he obviously has the soul of Gandalf. When Tolkien's son Christopher had to fill in the blank labelled "father's occupation" on his army induction form, he wrote "wizard". I'm sure Jim's students do the same.

Frodo is Pope John Paul the Great, the greatest man in the worst century in history, who carried more of the burden of the Ring than anyone else in the world.

And as Sam carried Frodo and the Ring for a little while up Mount Doom, Walter Hooper carried this burden for a split second when he visited the pope and received his blessing in the form of the laying on of the papal hands on his shoulders, Hooper said he felt the entire weight of the world in his body, which was suddenly on fire with unendurable pain and pressure. He looked up at the pope's eyes and saw the source of the pain there. The pope said, "I'm sorry, I didn't know that would happen", and took his hands, and the burden, off Walter's shoulders.

That happened only for a second. Walter was Sam for a second. There is a more enduring Sam. All his life, our Frodo was served by another Sam, whose two names are Ratzinger and Benedict. This Sam became Frodo's successor and then Mayor of the Shire.

Who is our Aragorn? Ronald Reagan comes to mind, but since Aragorn is also the *future* king, I hopefully assign the title to Mike Huckabee.[1] President Obama would then be Denethor, the steward whose proper job is to keep the throne warm for the king.

Gimli has to be Chuck Colson, that doughty culture warrior, dark of hue, square of shape, serious of voice, and adamant of will, swinging his orc-slaying intellectual axe in word and deed.

Legolas is Fr. Michael Scanlon, the elvish Saint Francis of Assisi, with that eternally young twinkle in his eye. He was able to pull off real feats of Elvish magic in Steubenville, which he turned into Rivendell.

Boromir is George H. W. Bush, a culture warrior on the right side who failed and fell but was nevertheless noble and heroic.

Finally, I give the names of Merry and Pippin to Pastor Tim Keller and Fr. Joseph Fessio.

The identity game can also be played for others beyond the Nine. Malcolm Muggeridge is surely Tom Bombadil. Arwen, in her expanded movie role of warrior, is Maggie Thatcher (in spirit, not in face, of course). Alice von Hilde-

---

[1] If anyone still has doubts about whether I have any prophetic gifts, this should resolve them. At least I resisted the temptation to update my picks. (Peter Kreeft, 2020).

brand is Galadriel. Faramir is Bill Donohue, or perhaps Randall Terry. Fangorn, Treebeard, is of course Tolkien himself. That's very obvious from his voice on the tape recording of the scene in the book where the hobbits meet him. Archbishop Weakland is our Saruman. Sauron is of course the Father of Lies, the Prince of the Power of the Airwaves, the media. Or perhaps the media is only the Mouth of Sauron, that awful figure at the Black Gate, the Lieutenant of Barad-dûr who has forgotten his own name. Or perhaps the media is Wormtongue, and Théoden is the Democratic Party. If so, then there is still hope of an exorcism by Gandalf. (Jim, where's your staff?)

And Gollum—well, alas, Gollum is Western civilization.

If we read Tolkien's masterpiece thoughtfully, we will find in its pages far more wartime wisdom than this little name game. *The Lord of the Rings* is not an allegory, of course, but it is a myth; and a myth is more, not less, than an allegory in its applicability, for a myth is universal, applicable to many situations, while an allegory is applicable to just one. The setting is neither mythical nor allegorical but literal. We still live in Tolkien's Middle Earth. We live literally in Tolkien's world. It is the only one we know, the one designed by God, the same God, the only God we know, and designed according to the same principles, the only principles we know, what Lewis called the Tao; and therefore it has the same truths embedded in all its events, especially its wars, including its culture wars. Here, too, victory depends on friendship and loyalty and courage and perseverance and gift-giving and sacrifice and promise-keeping more than on power or cleverness, control or foresight. And it depends on the foolishness of trusting great tasks to humble hobbits. After all, when God became a man, He became a humble hobbit. He became a Frodo. A Sam, in fact, a servant.

Some day perhaps someone will write a book about this strange philosophy of Tolkien. Perhaps they will call it *The Philosophy of Tolkien*. Perhaps some will actually read it. Perhaps they will even live it.

We must let C.S. Lewis speak now in what remains in this chapter.

One way we can do that is by listing the ten most important questions we need to answer if we are to win the culture war and by listing the ten books or articles that Lewis has given us to answer those questions.

To win any war, you need to know ten things.

First, you need to know that you are at war. If you blunder across battlefields sewing peace banners, mistaking bullets for butterflies, you will soon find yourself not in peace but in pieces.

Second, you need to know who your enemy is. If you fight civil wars against your friends while you are supposed to be together fighting your real enemy, he will win by the most efficient of all bits of military strategy, "divide and conquer".

Third, you need to know how big the war is. If you do not see the forces arrayed against you beyond the horizon, you will die like General Custer, whose last words were, "What Indians?"

Fourth, you need to know what the war is about, what you are fighting for. If you think "it's the economy, stupid", then like Marx you will sacrifice millions of human bodies and souls for the sake of the redistribution of dirty pieces of paper.

Fifth, you need to know what the enemy's strategy is. If you don't realize how strategic Little Round Top Hill is, you will lose Gettysburg, and if you don't catch spies like Klaus Fuchs in time, Russia will get the bomb.

Sixth, you need to cope with injuries. If you are surprised by suffering, by defeats, by casualties, and have no hospitals and no medicine for them, you will soon be depleted, both physically and emotionally.

Seventh, you need to identify the main battlefield, so you can send your crack troops there. If you let the enemy take over Washington D.C., while you are defending Alaska, you are the kind of person who will exchange two twenty-dollar bills for a ten.

Eighth, you need to know what weapon will win the war. If you neglect to re-forge the shards of Narsil and use the Palantir instead, you will end as a Denethor instead of an Aragorn.

Ninth, you need to know how to get and use this weapon. You don't win wars on paper, by dreaming about victory, or merely by *having* superior weapons if they lie rusting in your armory.

Tenth, you need to know that you *will* win; or at least you need to know that you will never, never, never, never give up.

Lewis teaches us every one of these essential lessons for our culture war.

First, he teaches us that we are at war in *The Abolition of Man*, one of the most important books of the last few centuries. The shocking title tells us what is at stake in this war—human nature itself. The death of God and His moral law, His Tao, necessarily entails the death of man, for man is God's image, and someone's image cannot long remain in a mirror after he himself disappears.

This book also tells us what kind of war this is—a spiritual war—and what its main battlefield is: the mind, schools, education, textbooks. When all our textbooks are Green Books, we will have turned into animals, in fact, geckos, tiny little green things. Kermit the Frog is wrong: it *is* easy being green. Geckos are nice. They make no trouble. But they are not men. They are Canadians.[2] America's best hope is the fact that our borders are not being invaded by Canadians but by Mexicans.

Second, Lewis identifies our enemy in *The Great Divorce* as well as *The Screwtape Letters*. It is, of course, our old friend the Devil and his War Room in Hell. If that is not true but only exaggeration or myth, then Jesus Christ was a fool and we'd better stop idealizing him and start ignoring him or correcting him or even sneering at him for sounding too much like a fire-breathing Texas preacher man.

Third, Lewis tells us how big the war is in his space trilogy. It's as big as space, as big as the cosmos. It's bigger than the world. Our culture war is only a footnote to the War in Heaven. The Apocalypse, the Book of Revelation, told us the same thing. But Lewis' space trilogy is more fun to read.

Fourth, Lewis tells us what the war is about, what it's for: eternal souls. He tells us this in *The Problem of Pain*:

> All your life an unattainable ecstasy has hovered just beyond the grasp of your consciousness. The day is coming when you will wake to find, beyond all hope, that you have attained it, or else, that it was within your reach and you have lost it forever.

And he tells us this in *Perelandra*:

> As there is one Face above all worlds merely to see which is irrevocable joy, so at the bottom of all worlds that face is waiting whose sight alone is the misery from which none who beholds it can recover. And though there seemed to be, and indeed were, a thousand roads by which a man

---

[2] Canadians are so nice they apologize for being so apologetic.

could walk through the world, there was not a single one which did not lead sooner or later either to the Beatific or the Miserific Vision.

And he tells us this in "The Weight of Glory", in one of the most stunning and quotable paragraphs ever written:

> The load, or weight, or burden of my neighbour's glory should be laid daily on my back, a load so heavy that only humility can carry it and the backs of the proud will be broken. . . . The dullest and most uninteresting person you talk to may one day be a creature which, if you saw it now, you would be strongly tempted to worship, or else a horror and a corruption such as you now meet, if at all, only in a nightmare. All day long we are, in some degree, helping each other to one or other of these destinations. . . . There are no *ordinary* people. You have never talked to a mere mortal. Nations, cultures, arts, civilizations—these are mortal, and their life is to ours as the life of a gnat. But it is immortals whom we joke with, work with, marry, snub, and exploit—immortal horrors or everlasting splendours.

That is what is at stake in this war. For this war is for souls, not just bodies. That's what culture is: culture is cultus, cultivation, the cultivation of souls, the farming of souls in the soil of society and its transformations of the material world, which is what we call civilization. Civilization is the body of culture; culture is the soul of civilization.

Fifth, Lewis reveals the Enemy's strategy in amazing and accurate detail in *The Screwtape Letters*. I think the lightness and wit of its style is the only reason this book is not yet classified with the spiritual classics of all time, with *The Imitation of Christ* and *The Introduction to the Devout Life* and *A Serious Call to the Devout Life* and *Abandonment to Divine Providence* and *The Practice of the Presence of God*. The content is all there, in very practical and concrete detail. All that's needed for *The Screwtape Letters* to be accepted by our literary Establishment is for someone with the imagination, verve, and style of Job's three friends or the author of an inter-office communications memo to translate it into long, dull, preachy platitudes. I suggest this task be assigned to ICEL, the International Commission on English in the Liturgy in the 1970s.

Sixth, *The Problem of Pain* and *A Grief Observed* give us a medical injury report and medicines for the injured soul, the first book on the philosophical, intellectual level and the second on the personal and emotional. There are thousands of imitations, but *The Problem of Pain* is simply the best book I know to give to anyone blocked from faith by apparently meaningless and unjust suffering, and *A Grief Observed* is the best book I know to give to any griever who respects tough-minded honesty . . .

Seventh, Lewis shows us where the main battlefield is—in the mind—in *The Abolition of Man* and also in exposing the philosophy of Weston in *Perelandra* and of the N.I.C.E., especially the philosopher Filostrato, in *That Hideous Strength*. The fact that philosophy is required in fewer than 5 percent of American colleges and the fact that most philosophers in secular schools are atheists or agnostics show how clever the Enemy is in choosing his battles.

Here is an alternative scenario: Though abstractly, the main battlefield is philosophy; concretely, the main battlefield is sex. The main motor for a general moral relativism is sexual relativism and the Sexual Revolution. Most of the rest of traditional morality is still in place. We never speak of a justice revolution or a money revolution or a truth-telling revolution, but we all know there has been a sexual revolution. All the most controversial, radical, and hot-button issues today are about sex: cohabitation, abortion, homosexuality, contraception, divorce, feminism. The Sexual Revolution is far more radical than any political revolution in history. Politics is only water off the duck's back, but sex is inside the duck.

Another prophet, Chesterton, said almost a century ago that the great evil of the future would come, not from Moscow, but from Manhattan, and he identified it as an attack, not on theology, but on morality, especially sexual morality. Lewis clarifies that subject with wonderful simplicity in the "Eros" chapter in *The Four Loves* and in the simple little article "We Have No Right to Happiness", which was, providentially, the last thing he ever wrote, published posthumously.

Eighth, Lewis tells us what the winning weapon is in *Mere Christianity*, which is the best, most persuasive, clearest, simplest, most direct, most ecumenical, and above all most Christocentric introduction to Christianity I have ever read outside the New Testament. The one weapon guaranteed to win is of course Christ Himself.

Lewis' supreme literary achievement was to do in *The Chronicles of Narnia* what Dorothy Sayers said could never be done: portray Christ as a compelling fictional character, by removing Him from the familiarity of humanity and earth to the fictionality of leoninity and Narnia. On earth, lions eat the body of Christ, Christians; in Narnia, the lion *is* Christ. When we go to Narnia, we can actually feel Christ there, and we can feel toward Him what we should feel on earth but can't: the awe, the wonder, the wildness, the hot, searing love that makes men martyrs, because we know He really *is* Narnian and leonine and not American and politically correct.

Ninth, Lewis shows us how to get this winning weapon

in *Letters to Malcolm* and *Reflections on the Psalms*. It's prayer. Just ask. It's so simple.

Finally, he gives us his (and God's) prognosis of victory. This is suggested in a few passages, at the end of *The Abolition of Man*, about the new, redeemed science and in *Miracles*: in chapter 5's supposition that divine providence is allowing the death of supernaturalist traditionalism only to spur us all on to recapture it ourselves and in that book's masterful concluding chapter entitled "Miracles of the New Creation"; but most clearly at the end of *The Last Battle*, which is his version of the Apocalypse. (Is it sinful to enjoy reading his version better than God's? If so, I offer a Very Short Act of Contrition: Oops.)

Mention of *The Last Battle* and Narnia reminds us that every piece of fiction Lewis ever wrote was about spiritual and (often physical) warfare—as is the whole Bible and three quarters of the psalms. So I will now take one specific lesson from each of his eleven novels, namely, the seven Narnia chronicles, the space trilogy, and *Till We Have Faces*. These eleven points are not necessarily the main points of each book, but each is a helpful answer to how to win our culture wars.

The Lion, the Witch and the Wardrobe tells us that any one of us, including children, can walk through something as ordinary as a wardrobe and find ourselves in a world where lions and witches battle in a real world war. Frodo Baggins found the same thing at the door of Bag End: a road to Rivendell, Moria, Lorien, and Mordor—there and back again. Be ready; your recruiting officer comes as a thief in the night.

Prince Caspian shows the danger of chronological snobbery and the preciousness of tradition, of memory, of ancestors. We can't win without them. (This is the same thing *The*

Lord of the Rings shows on nearly every page: it is saturated with the past, like the air just before a hurricane, when the humidity is 100 percent.) Our marching orders are not to "Create new values" but to "Hold fast." This is supremely shocking to the salient superstition of the Enlightenment, but Eternity's impregnation of Time is not just future but past; that is why it is already present.

The Voyage of the Dawn Treader complements this traditionalism with the futurism of hope, in fact, of *Sehnsucht*, of longing, of Joy. On the other side of the battlefield is the promised land of world's end; and the world is flat—in time, if not in space. (*The Voyage of the Dawn Treader* images this truth of the end of time by the end of space, where the sky meets the sea, Heaven meets Earth.) What motivates us to fight this war is love of our true Homeland and our Heavenly Lover. The only way there is through many obstacles and strange islands, and we need Reepicheep and his sword on board our ship. And we need Reepicheep inside us, since this ship is the soul.

The Horse and His Boy shows us that animals are also part of this war. Lewis shows us horses that talk to remind us that we talkers are more like horses than like angels. They are part of our family, and we are part of theirs.

The Magician's Nephew shows us the danger of hubris, of becoming an Uncle Andrew, and the danger of Eve-like curiosity, which can summon a Witch by striking a bell; and the power of music, which is the very language of creation. (Remember the battle of the two musics in Tolkien's *Silmarillion*.)

The Silver Chair shows us how to escape our addictions and hallucinations: the way Prince Rilian did, by the politically incorrect contradicting of the Underground Witch's propaganda, which is at once philosophical, musical, and pharmacological. Sometimes the only way to do this is by the courage to embrace suffering, as Puddleglum did in stamping on the witch's fire with his foot. (Remember Samuel Johnson's great wisdom: I know of no thought that more wonderfully clarifies a man's mind than the thought that tomorrow morning he will be hanged . . . or diagnosed with cancer.)

And *The Last Battle* teaches us to beware imitations and apes. There are many lion skins worn by apes out there, many fake Messiahs, new Christianities, shifts and shufflers and nuancers and necromancers. Not all those within our castle walls are allies, and not all those without are enemies. We have allies outside Narnia: they are anyone whose name is Emeth, faithful and true. When we see the heretic Muhammad and the bishop Judas Iscariot in pitched battle, let us not hesitate to fight with Muhammad.

Out of the Silent Planet reminds us that the whole cosmos is full, not empty: full of life and light and spirit; that the cosmos is on our side; that evil is a small and local thing, like that single star Sam saw in Mordor that smote his heart with hope; that this is the only silent planet and that we must poke our head through its clouds and listen to the music of the spheres.

And *Perelandra* plays this angel music. The Great Dance, at the end, is certainly the most beautiful and the most mystical thing Lewis ever wrote; and that is, ultimately, what we are fighting for; and what we are fighting against is not a man but an un-man. We are like Dr. Van Helsing and our enemy is Dracula: not flesh and blood, but principalities and powers. Our lord is Christ, and our enemy is the Antichrist, not suicide bombers or George Soros or Ted Turner or Walt Disney, or even the Democratic Party.

That Hideous Strength warns us of the alliance the enemy has forged between evil technology and evil mysticism. Mark Studdock's "objective room" is a Deconstructionist paradise. (It actually exists, on the campus of the University of Kansas.) But with the help of some Merlins and Mr. Bultitudes, we can help the powers of Deep Heaven pull down the new tower of Babel.

Finally, *Till We Have Faces*, Lewis' most profound—and best written—book, shows us who we are (Orual *is* Ungit) and how only the Way of Exchange can save us, where Orual and Psyche work out each other's salvation. If we are not willing to die for each other, if our human loves are jealous, the Enemy has split our ranks and split our happiness. Only the unity of Orual and Psyche can bring about the union of Psyche and Cupid. Horizontal unity is the other side of vertical unity. Only when the Communion of Saints perfects Heaven's society can we attain the Beatific Vision, which in Scripture is always corporate, not private.

The truths Tolkien and Lewis tell us are perennial and, therefore, current; universal and, therefore, local. They apply to culture wars in first-century Rome as well as twenty-first-century America. Lewis was utterly up to date because he did not waste time on ephemera like newspapers. He read, not the *Times*, but the eternities. Because that's where the war started and that's where it is being strategized and that's where it will end. Paradoxically, at the same time, it begins and ends at the front door of Bag End, in Hobbiton, in the Shire. For that is where eternity intersects time, like the two bars of the Cross.

Christ steered past the dead past of the repentant thief on the cross and saw only the Paradise in his soul in the living present, because Christ lived in the holy Now. Let us do the same.

And if we do, if we live in the holy Now, we will know that we have done enough thinking and speaking. Now let us march.

10

Heroes

All stories have protagonists. Great ones have heroes.

The greatest stories are about the greatest heroes. Great stories need great heroes to make them great stories, and great heroes need great stories to be in to make them great heroes.

Many years ago, our babysitter approached me with her high-school assignment: she had to get twenty people's answers to the question, "Who are your heroes?" So I spoke for three minutes into her tape recorder and said some obvious things about Jesus, Socrates, and my father. She was effusively grateful, and I said something like "Just because I'm a philosopher, that doesn't mean I have the best answers." And she replied, "You're the only one of the twenty people I interviewed who answered the question. Everybody else said they didn't have any heroes anymore, that heroes are kid stuff." At first I felt embarrassed at my answer, but then I felt grateful.

Is our world a world without heroes? If so, why? If not, who?

Obviously, we can't answer this question unless we know what heroes are. So, logically, we should first define our term.

But I will do something better than that. We often have a deep, unconscious, intuitive understanding of something that we can't clearly define, like time or being or beauty. So I want to explore that.

I think we know what heroes are because we know what a world without heroes would be like. It would be like *Brave New World*.

We are moving closer and closer to *Brave New World*. But we're not quite there yet. It's still science fiction, not science fact. It's a cautionary tale, a dystopia, not a utopia—except to a class of my students in the sixties, who misunderstood it as a utopia. Worse, they loved it and couldn't understand why anyone wouldn't want to live in it. My hope for humanity's future comes from the fact that most students don't misinterpret it that badly anymore.

Most of us have sports heroes. Are they real heroes?

Can actors be heroes? Favorite singers? Fictional characters? Cartoon characters? Superheroes?

Do we love them because we don't have real heroes anymore? Or do we love them for exactly the opposite reason: because we do still believe in real heroes?

Perhaps only moral heroes are real heroes. Anyone lacking in wisdom, courage, self-control, justice, or charity is not a hero. Fools, cowards, addicts, tyrants, or egotists can't be heroes.

Perhaps we can answer our first question, whether we live in a world without heroes, by listing the preconditions for heroes, the aspects of a world view that make heroism possible. (These are not the attributes of heroes themselves. We listed a number of them already. Those are moral virtues. These are philosophical beliefs.)

A hero is someone who not only has virtue but who is publicly admired for it. Socrates had virtue, but Athens did not admire him for it; they killed him for it. He was not a hero to Athens, though he was to Plato and to us. Jesus was not a hero to the Sanhedrin or to the Pharisees or to the Romans or to the mob that shouted "crucify Him!" But he was to his disciples and to us.

But Athens and Jerusalem had heroes—Pericles, for instance, and Moses. For they had the philosophical presuppositions for heroism. They had the categories. They just didn't think Socrates and Jesus fit those categories. What is questionable about our world is whether we even have the categories. Perhaps we do. Let's see. What are the categories? What are the preconditions for heroism?

I see at least seven:

1. hierarchy;
2. teleology, purpose, or design;
3. a Tao, or natural law;
4. absolutism, some absolute that can elicit infinite passion, an "all-or-nothing";
5. free will;
6. honor; and
7. suffering, poverty, and death.

These are only *presuppositions* of heroism. Their presence does not guarantee the presence of heroes, but their absence does guarantee the absence of heroes. They are necessary causes, not sufficient causes.

Let's see why this is so, for each one, and let's ask whether we still have each one.

1. Heroes are superior to ordinary people, so the idea of heroism is hierarchical. We usually misunderstand hierarchy as something political, as a class system. We project our human politics onto the cosmos. And we don't do monarchies or aristocracies; we don't do hierarchy; we do democracy. But nature is not democratic, nature is hierarchical. People are higher than animals. People have duties to be kind to

animals, but animals don't have rights as people do. If dogs have rights, then so do fleas.

2. Objective purpose, or teleology, is necessary for heroes because a hero has to fulfill some such destiny, fate, or purpose. We no longer use teleological explanations in science, and that's just as right as no longer having monarchies or aristocracies in politics. But there is more to reality than what science sees. Astronomically speaking, man is insignificant, but astronomically speaking, man is the astronomer. Of course, there is "intelligent design", but that's not a scientific category. It's data, not for the senses, but for the mind, and it's not *mathematical* mind-data but *understanding* mind-data. Design is a category computers can't understand, but computer designers can. Unfortunately, we tend to assume that if it's not scientific, it's not objective, so we reduce design and purpose and teleology to something subjective and psychological. So we reduce objective goodness to subjective, personal values. (Did Moses come down Sinai with ten values?)

3. A world without objective moral values, without the natural law, is a world without heroes. Only an objective morality, not a subjective morality, can be the frame around the picture of the plot of a life. *Macbeth* is a great drama because Shakespeare believed the Christian moral frame. It's a story of damnation, of a man who went morally insane. That's the point of his famous speech about life being "a tale told by an idiot, full of sound and fury, signifying nothing". But Faulkner, in his classic *The Sound and the Fury*, showed us what life looks like without the frame. Someone like Macbeth tells the story (actually five people); there's no frame in which to judge truth against falsity, good against evil. Goethe did something like the same thing with the old Faust story, which was a Christian story of damnation until

Goethe made it a post-Christian story of personal integra-
tion and fulfillment. Faust integrates his inner Satan and his
inner God together, at the price of morality. Goethe drops
the moral frame that condemns him, damns him. The frame
is the natural moral law. Insofar as modernity has dropped
that frame, it has made heroism impossible.

And that is probably the most radical and distinctive difference between modern Western civilization and every other
civilization in history. We are the first culture in history
without a Tao, at least in the minds of its mind-molders, its
teachers, both formal and informal, both in education and
in popular media. And what is in the mind of the teacher
will soon be in the mind of the student. That's why we are
increasingly becoming a world without heroes.

4. A hero has an absolute. That's why he has all-or-
nothing passion for it. But we don't do absolutes anymore.
It's not that we've disproved them; we just don't like them.
They make us uncomfortable, and we worship our comfort bubble. We fear absolutism more than we fear damnation. (Indeed, we fear the idea of damnation more than we
fear damnation, because the idea sounds far too absolutistic.) We confuse absolutism with fundamentalism and fanaticism, and those are our two new F-words. We tolerate
anything but intolerance. Tolerance is the last virtue that is
still left after you have lost all your principles.

I think this explains our fear of Islam. I think there's hid-
den envy in it. "The lady doth protest too much, methinks."
Of course there is much not to envy in Islam: terrorism, lack
of respect for human life, for women, for reason, and for
freedom. But Muslims are almost always genuinely moral,
though narrow. And therefore they have heroes and saints.
Because they have spines. We don't. We are jellyfish; they
are skeletons. We need an exchange program to get the two

parts of humanity back together, the bones and the flesh. We need to rent a fleet of airplanes and ship them all our pop psychologists so they can ship us back all their fiery mullahs.

Without religion, without an infinite reality, how can you have infinite passion? And without infinite passion, how can you have heroism? If there is a Heaven and a Hell, life is a battlefield. If not, life is a hot tub. There are no heroes in hot tubs.

We quite naturally prefer hot tubs to battlefields. But we're wistful. We don't admit it, but we envy those who still have battlefields. Especially spiritual battlefields, which the Koran calls "the greater jihad". And that's why our society discriminates only against religious believers, is intolerant only to the intolerant. Like Merseault in Camus' *The Stranger*: he is a totally passionless man whose only passion is directed against the priest who tells him he ought to have passion about his salvation, about Heaven or Hell. That's us, that's modern man. Only one absolute: no absolutes, please. No heroes. They're too *primitive*.

5. Free will is obviously necessary for heroism because robots can't be heroes. But we've questioned free will and embraced, instead, another kind of freedom: autonomy. That's the adolescent's favorite kind of freedom: "don't tread on me", "get on with your own life, leave me alone." The two freedoms are in tension, because free will is the foundation for moral responsibility, and moral responsibility means we are *not* autonomous but under authority, the authority of the moral law. If there's free will and moral responsibility and a real moral law, a Tao, then you can have both heroes and villains, you can have both praise and blame, you can have both glory and guilt. If not, not. It's a package deal; you can't have the heights without the depths, heroes

without villains, Heaven without Hell. So if you refuse to have villains, you can't have heroes, and if you don't fear damnation, you can't hope for salvation, because damnation is what salvation is salvation from.

Free will sees freedom as a means. Autonomy sees it as an end. Free will sees freedom as a relative good, relative to The Good. Autonomy sees it as an absolute good. The question that distinguishes the two concepts of freedom is: Can you have too much freedom? If you suddenly become very rich and very famous, and as a result you have the money for all the drugs and prostitutes you want, so you scramble your soul and bottle your brains and lose your life, didn't you have too much freedom?

Isn't freedom almost the same thing as power? If you're in prison or in a wheelchair, you have less of it. But we all know that power tends to corrupt, that too much power corrupts. Why don't we ever say that about freedom?

Freedom of autonomy, at its height, demands the freedom to create your own values. Free will, on the other hand, presupposes objective values, Tao, or moral law, because without a moral law to define good and evil, you can't have a meaningful free choice between good and evil.

The only way you can combine the two freedoms is by being a moral hero, a saint, because then your will, by your own free choice, is totally one with God's will, and God's will alone is autonomous.

Most psychologists and sociologists are determinists; that is, they do not believe in free will. Science requires causal explanations, and the pressure to make these two sciences into respectable sciences, fully scientific sciences, leads their practitioners to search for causal explanations of apparently free human choices. But if our choices are not self-caused but caused by other forces, whether inside us (heredity) or outside us (environment)—if they are not merely *conditioned* by these forces but causally *determined*, then they are not free. Our wills are just pencils in the hands of these impersonal forces. We are not to blame for anything: the conflicts between ourselves and our societies, between our ids and our superegos, is to blame; or else the selfish genes we have inherited from our father who art on earth, King Kong instead of King God; or else the historically retrograde capitalist competitive class system is to blame. It's Adam and Eve all over again. Adam blamed Eve, and Eve blamed the Devil.

Blaming women and demons is definitely out of fashion today, but blaming impersonal forces is not. It gets us off the hook. And, therefore, it ultimately puts God on the hook, since He is the ultimate first cause of all other forces except our own free choices. Thus the popularity of the apparently scientific philosophies of exculpation (de-guiltifying), especially Freud, Darwin, and Marx. All three are part of the same strategy we used in Eden: to explain away responsibility, guilt, and free will. And the result of success in *that* is the failure of heroes, of drama, and, ultimately, of all meaningful storytelling. No determinist ever wrote a great story.

6. Honor is a sixth prerequisite for heroes. It is part of their motivation and of their identity and definition. Honor is the index of heroism, the special light that lights them up, so to speak. But the word "honor" is hardly ever heard anymore in our world outside the Marine Corps, unless it is in scorn. Or if we use it, we reduce it to something relative, changeable, and subjective: society's acceptance. We don't distinguish *deserving* honor from *getting* it. Thus our rap stars who exalt rape and murder get more honor than our saints.

David Riesman, in his '50s sociological classic *The Lonely Crowd*, marveled at the 180-degree change of meaning in our concept of honor. All previous societies honored the hero for excellence, for being better, for being different from the crowd. But modern society is so anti-hierarchical that it honors you for *not* being different, for being one of the crowd, for getting your meaning and your values, not from higher sources, but from other people, from popularity. The ancient hero was either the "tradition-directed man", if he obeyed the tradition heroically, or the "inner-directed man", if he transcended and critiqued his society's traditions; but the modern conformist is the "other-directed man", taking his values, standards, meanings, and purposes from fads and fashions, from the *Zeitgeist*, the spirit of the times.

Modern men have rejected the authority of their heroes, like sheep rejecting their shepherds; but this did not make them all shepherds. Sheep without shepherds are still sheepish. They just move differently: instead of walking in a line following their shepherd, they move in aimless circles. In such a sheepish place, there are no heroes. There are only very nice, polite sheep. If you want to see an advanced case of men turning into sheep, visit Canada. I think Canada can be saved only by massive immigration from the lower east side of New York City.

7. Poverty, suffering, and death are our last prerequisite for heroes.

Poverty because riches remove uncertainty, unpredictability, and adventure. Chesterton defines an adventure as nothing but "an inconvenience rightly considered" and an inconvenience as "only an adventure wrongly considered". Wealth gives you control over inconvenience and, therefore, the abolition of adventure. To see this, read Solzhenitsyn's 1978 Harvard commencement address. He said, in effect, that Russians may be more wicked than Americans, but they're a lot more interesting because they suffer poverty, injustice, torture, and oppression. People in a bubble are boring.

You have to *have* suffering to have an interesting story, but you have to *accept* suffering when it comes in order to have heroism. There is little or no room for dramatic, interesting stories in our pleasure bubbles, our Brave New Worlds. And there is little room in our consciousness anymore for the concept of "mortification" of our natural selfish urges, of asceticism or deliberate self-sacrifice. Mother Teresa's Missionaries of Charity have drawn dozens, hundreds of women to her deeply and mysteriously joyful work in America, but very few of them are Americans.

Death is, of course, the most dramatic event of all. It is the frame that makes life interesting. When I picked ten films on which to concentrate in my Philosophy in Cinema class, I thought I picked them based merely on how great I thought they were, but I discovered that every one of them was about death. If "man's conquest of nature" finds its apotheosis in the conquest of death, nature's trump card, by inventing artificial immortality by genetic engineering (which most geneticists consider theoretically possible), *Brave New World* will be here.

But can ordinary people be heroes? Even if we can't, we can revere them, tell stories about them, and thus help others to revere them. And the first step to becoming a hero yourself is revering heroism in others.

And we *can* be heroes. In fact, we must. The whole point of the greatest book of the twentieth century, according to its author, is to show the mutual dependence of little heroes and big heroes, of hobbits and warriors, wizards, and elves. The high heroes fight and work and sacrifice for the low ones, the little ones; but they cannot succeed unless the little ones do their part. Middle Earth was saved by hobbits.

The greatest hero in history was not a warrior or a wizard or an elf (though He had all those powers, if He had
wanted to use them); He was like a little hobbit. He was
a poor, obscure carpenter-rabbi who was born in a stable,
never wrote a book, never traveled from His tiny country,
and never entered politics. He was crucified as a criminal.
He was, by all worldly standards, a spectacular failure, like
one of Gandalf's firecrackers, that gave itself up, burned
brightly for a moment, and then was no more. And yet He
is so real and so alive that He split history in half forever,
like a coconut, into B.C. and A.D., and inserted eternity into
the crack. Why? Because He told us the only two things
we need to know: the identity of the only two persons we
will never, ever be able to avoid, for all eternity: God and
ourselves. The favorite quotation of the greatest man in the
worst century in history is the one about what He did, from
the documents of Vatican II: Christ revealed not only God
to man, but also man to himself. He showed us what we
all are in the eyes of our Author: heroes because we can
become one with the one complete Hero. And He did this
in story form, by starring in a movie, the greatest story ever
told. Our job is now to join His Central Casting for that
movie.

11

What Is a Liberal?

Bottom line conclusion first: I don't know. I feel like the geriatric Italian paterfamilias in *Moonstruck*: "I'm so confused."

I find hardly any philosophical or ideological term more confusing than the term "liberalism". I used to call myself a liberal, back in the sixties. I now call myself a conservative. But I haven't changed my mind on a single issue. The labels have changed.

Here are some of the issues on which the labels have changed and what I believed and still believe about them. I trusted the doves more than the hawks, especially about the Vietnam War. I approved the Civil Rights movement and Martin Luther King's so-called radicalism or progressivism. I distrusted big government, big business, and big military. I trusted common sense, common people, little people, middle-class people, and families and distrusted so-called "experts". I believed that the one thing common to all of the most idiotic ideas I had ever heard was that only a Ph.D. could possibly believe them. I believed that "small is beautiful" and approved cutting back on our luxurious lifestyle for the sake of environmental stewardship. I thought the individual was infinitely more important than the collective. I distrusted the expansion of government. Above all, I believed in the natural law, a higher law than the laws of the State, and I approved protests against the laws of the State in the name of that higher law, the law that declared that all human lives, not just some, had intrinsic and nonnegotiable value, from the womb to the tomb. All those causes were labeled "liberal" fifty years ago. They're labeled "conservative" today. Whatever happened to the labels?

I speak only of America. Europe to me is a koan puzzle, an apostasy, and a death wish. And Canada is a sheepfold where the sheep politely and voluntary line up for the slaughterhouse.

I remember reading a poll (I couldn't find the actual source, so this is only anecdotal) that polled Ivy League professors fifty years ago and found that over 80 percent had voted Republican. The same poll recently showed that over 90 percent now vote Democrat.

This is quite a puzzle. Philosophers love intellectual puzzles, so I tried to solve this one, and here is the solution I came up with. It's not the whole story, but I think it's the heart of the story.

Historically, liberalism used to mean the tendency to trust individuals more and governments less; now it means the opposite. Why? Here's a clue: Because governments used to be more religious than individuals, and now they are less, just as the clergy and the theologians used to believe more than the laity, but in the second half of the twentieth century they came to believe less.

Religion, after all, has always been mankind's deepest divide, their most passionate loyalty. It has made more of a difference to more lives, throughout all history, than anything else. Religion always claims absoluteness. If there's anything liberals hate today, it's absolutes. So of course they fear religion—real religion, as distinct from the mild dose of it that is the new, safe, politically correct religion of left-wing politics, the religion that is the most effective inoculation against the real thing that the Devil ever invented. In Massachusetts, we Catholics distinguish these two religions by saying that Kennedy Catholics vastly outnumber Catholic Kennedys.

Religion believes in a higher law, a natural law. Some non-religious thinkers believe in a natural moral law, too, but they are rare. For most people, religious and moral absolutes go together. This is simply a sociological fact, whether or not reason alone without religious faith can prove the existence of the natural law (as I believe it can) and whether or not a nation can succeed if it is based on a natural law without appealing to revealed religion (as America's founders hoped it could, and so do I).

Fifty years ago, liberals and Democrats were basing their opposition to segregation and the Vietnam War on natural law and demanding changes in positive law on that basis. The Republicans tended to establishment pragmatism. Today, it is conservatives and Republicans who are basing their opposition to abortion, assisted suicide, and gay marriage on natural law. It is the Democrats and so-called liberals who will not tolerate natural law absolutes because they call that intolerant. Fifty years ago, liberals trusted religious individuals against irreligious governments; now, they trust irreligious governments against religious individuals. The Obama administration showed an astonishing incomprehension of the very meaning of religious conscience in reneging on its promise to Catholic institutions to give them a conscience-clause exception about having to pay for abortifacient contraceptives and was genuinely surprised when all the bishops said No, this is a line in the sand that we simply cannot erase. This new kind of liberalism is a 180-degree turn, almost like a conversion from Red Sox fan to Yankee fan.

I will now ask you to allow me to ignore everything I have just said, not because it is false, but because it is about the confusing shadows in Plato's cave (that's where politics is: in the cave), and I will ask you to try to climb out of the cave with me into the realm of pure Platonic Forms, time-less truths rather than historical ideologies. What should the word "liberal" mean if we think and speak clearly?

By definition, it has to do with liberty. In order to think clearly about political liberty, we need first to think clearly about human liberty, since politics is made of humans, made by humans, and made for humans. All government, not just democracy, is of the people, by the people, and for the people. The material cause, the "of", and the efficient cause, the "by", and the final cause, the "for", of all human government are human beings.

I assume, therefore, that John Rawls, the most prominent philosophical liberal of our time, is very fundamentally wrong when he calls for government without any "meta-narrative" or philosophical assumptions about the nature, purpose, and destiny of man. How can we govern human beings if we do not know what human beings are and what they are for? That is like a zookeeper trying to govern the monkey cage without knowing the difference between a monkey and an alligator or between a monkey and a man. (Actually, I think the majority of scientists today know less about this than ordinary uneducated people do. Not less detail, of course, but less of a "big picture", a "metanarrative", a philosophy.)

I assume, then, that Justice Anthony Kennedy's famous "mystery" passage is not the wisest but the most foolish, idiotic, and even insane thing ever written by a Supreme Court justice: that "At the heart of liberty is the right to define one's own concept of existence, of meaning, of the universe, and of the mystery of human life." This amounts to saying to our Creator and Designer, "Move over, you're sitting in my seat."

I would like to compare this famous passage with another famous passage, written by another famous and influential amateur philosopher named Benito Mussolini, in which he affirms the very same moral and metaphysical relativism:

> Everything I have said and done in these last years is relativism . . . if relativism signifies contempt for fixed categories and men who claim to be the bearers of an objective, immortal truth . . . then there is nothing more relativistic than Fascistic attitudes and activity. . . . From the fact that all ideologies are of equal value, that all ideologies are mere fictions, the modern relativist infers that everybody has the right to create for himself his own ideology and to attempt to enforce it with all the energy of which he is capable.[1]

In comparing these two quotations I challenge you to find any significant difference between the premises, or world view, of these two thinkers; and then I ask you how Kennedy could possibly avoid the logical conclusion that Mussolini quite logically derives from this common premise, a conclusion that Kennedy would want to avoid. Or would he? Kennedy's conclusion in *Casey v. Planned Parenthood* is that since the meaning of life, and therefore the value of life, is relative, it's OK to murder any innocent unborn human beings simply because you don't want them to live for personal or sexual reasons; and Mussolini draws the exact same conclusion regarding born human beings that you don't want to live because of racial or political reasons. The similarity is more important than the difference. The common

[1] Benito Mussolini, *Diuturna: scritti politici*, (Milan: Imperia, 1924), 374–77.

premises are more important than the different conclusions. Because there is nothing in principle to prevent us from deriving Mussolini's conclusions from Kennedy's premises if we want to.

What does this have to do with liberty and liberalism? In order to define liberalism, which is about liberty, we must define the thing that has liberty, the human being. My point against Kennedy, and Rawls is that it is impossible to have a political system, a government, without some philosophy of man, whether explicit or implicit, conscious or unconscious, rational or emotional, constitutional or fashionable, objective or subjective, permanent like a touchstone or shifting like a chameleon, set in stone or ink out there in the public domain like a Bible or subject to fads and fashions as dictated by popular media or political propagandists.

Therefore, to define political liberalism, we must define human liberty, and to define human liberty, we must define human beings—or, to use the old, inclusive language, "man".

First, man is soul as well as body. Materialism makes liberty impossible. If man has no spiritual soul, he has no liberty, for matter has no liberty. What we mean by liberty is *not* the unpredictability, randomness, and indeterminateness of subatomic particles.

Second, if man has no liberty of will, no free will, then any higher liberty is impossible, for everything that happens to him will be forced upon him from within (heredity) or without (environment) rather than attained by his own choice, like the so-called liberty of a baseball to fall to the ground once the hand of the outfielder who interferes with its fall by trying to catch it juggles it and drops it. This is the only "liberty" allowed by materialists like Hobbes.

Third, the higher liberty, to which the lower liberty of free will is a means, is moral liberty, not merely emotional liberty. It is not just freedom from unhappiness, but freedom from inhumanness; not just freedom from physical evil, but freedom from moral evil; not just freedom from suffering, but freedom from badness. What I called the lower liberty, free will, could be called negative freedom, freedom *from* determinism. The higher liberty could be called positive freedom, freedom *for*, freedom to attain the end and purpose of your existence. Augustine called these two freedoms "*liberum arbitrium*" and "*libertas*", free choice and liberty.

But this higher positive freedom, liberty to attain our end, means nothing if there is no such thing as our end, our real, objectively true end rather than merely whatever subjective end we want, whether it is saintliness or Satanism, charity or cannibalism.

The question of ends is unavoidable. Every association of human beings, from pragmatic alliances to hunt wooly mammoths to philosophical choices about a nation's constitution, must agree about the end of human life, at least in part, at least implicitly. If the end of man is to be eaten by wooly mammoths rather than to eat them, we do not hunt them. And if the end of man is not to discover but to create for himself his own meaning and end, as Kennedy and Mussolini say, then we do not write a Declaration of Independence that begins with words like these: "We hold these truths to be self-evident: that all men are created equal; that they are endowed by their Creator with certain inalienable rights; that among these are life, liberty and the pursuit of happiness. That to secure these rights, governments are instituted among men."

This is the most well-known and well-loved document in American history. The second most well-known and well-loved document in American history is Lincoln's Gettysburg Address. What Lincoln said there applies still today with as much urgency as it applied then. Only the numbers have changed, and the identity of those whose liberty is being fought over. Then it was the born; now it is the unborn:

> Four score and seven years ago our fathers brought forth on this continent a new nation, conceived in liberty and dedicated to the proposition that all men are created equal. Now we are engaged in a great civil war, testing whether that nation, or any nation so conceived and so dedicated, can long endure. . . . It is for us the living to be dedicated here to . . . the great task remaining before us . . . that we here highly resolve that these dead shall not have died in vain—that this nation, under God, shall have a new birth of freedom.

The original version of the Declaration of Independence read "property" in place of "the pursuit of happiness". America has faced three great enemies of liberty: communism, slavery, and abortion. Communism denied the right to property. Slavery denied the right to liberty. Abortion denies the right to life. The right to life is the most fundamental right of all, for if you are denied the right to life, you are denied all other rights as well. We have won two of these three wars against the enemies of liberty. We have struck out two of our enemy's three batters. The third enemy of liberty—the most important liberty of all—is now dug in at the plate. If we do not strike him out, we lose the whole game. With our lower liberty, free choice, we must now choose for or against our higher liberty: Do we choose Abraham Lincoln or Anthony Kennedy? Liberty is still a baby historically, still in process of being born. Do we choose death or life for this baby? How dare you call yourself a "liberal" if you answer "death", if you become a Caesar and put your thumb down to this little gladiator?

Whatever is the meaning and end of human life and whether or not a nation must have some public answer to that question, you cannot call yourself a defender of liberty if the liberty you defend is the liberty of some men to rob, enslave, or kill others. Communism, slavery, and abortion deny to their victims property, liberty, and life. The heart of liberalism is to side with the victim rather than with the victimizer. Please be a liberal. Please have a heart.

12

What Is the Key to a Good Society?

Let's start with some basic philosophy. Some philosophical anthropology, a philosophy of human nature.

Some things are wholly natural to man, like sexuality, socialization, language, technology, and play. Some things are artificial, like society's expectations about the differences in dress between males and females, the laws Congress chooses to enact, the English language, Facebook, the game of baseball.

All things that are natural to man (that is, conducive to the flourishing of human nature) are good. The things that are artificial are neutral. Things that are neutral can be used for good or evil. Natural things can also be used for evil as well as for good, but they are also good in themselves, so they have to be perverted before they can be used for evil. A weapon is neutral and can be used for or against a robbery, but sexuality is good in itself. That's why its perversions are even more serious than perversions of neutral things. Things like sex, intelligence, and free will are ontologically very good because they were invented by God as part of human nature; and they can be morally very good or very evil, depending on human choice. They can do immense good or immense harm to the doer, to the other person, and to the whole society.

Freedom and power are also morally neutral, though they are natural to man, not artificial, and therefore ontologically good. Freedom means the absence of determinism. It means almost the same thing as power. It is like a vacuum: the absence of matter. It can be filled with good stuff or with bad stuff. It is like an exorcised soul or an empty house. What makes it good or bad is whether the stuff you put into it is good or bad, whether the people who use it are good or bad morally. What makes both freedom and power good or bad is not how much of it there is. However, in a given situation, like how much freedom you as parents grant to your kids to make choices that you don't control, you can make mistakes in either direction, mistakes being dependent on the particular situation, especially how morally mature your kids are.

Government is a kind of power, and government can increase its power over people by things like taxation, Prohibition, or compulsory education; or it can withdraw its power and grant people more freedom by not imposing things like these. As with parents, governments are good or bad, not because they have too much or too little power, but because the people who are being ruled are good or bad people and use the power the government lets them have well or badly. In Heaven, there will be no need for civil government at all because everyone will be saintly and wise; in prisons and insane asylums, there is need for an almost totalitarian level of government.

Socialism is an economic system in which the government has more economic power, especially power to equalize wealth. Capitalism is a system in which the government has less economic power and relies on a free market.

Pure socialism is totally unworkable because without private property and the ability to increase personal wealth, without the profit motive, industry does not exist. If you equalized the wealth of all seven billion people on earth, by force, and kept the level equal, by force, each individual would have about $13,000 and *always* have $13,000. What would they do with it? What would happen tomorrow morning? Nothing. No one would employ anyone else, because employers have to have more wealth than employees. For there to be any economic progress, there has to be the hope of profit, and for there to be any hope of profit, the haves and the have nots have to be different.

Capitalism both presupposes (as a cause or precondition) and fosters (as an effect or natural result) ambition, which is a form of desire. Ambition, like power, is neutral: it can be good or bad. We can have good or bad desires. Unjust and uncharitable desires are bad; just and charitable desires are good. If the people in a society are more good than evil, if their desires and ambitions are more just than unjust and more charitable than competitively selfish, then capitalism will work for that society. Insofar as the people's desires are evil, that is, unjust and selfish, there is need for governmental force to correct or deter this. So there need to be some parts of socialism in a capitalist society, such as medical, food, and educational safety nets for the poor and a graduated income tax, since in capitalism the rich naturally get richer, and if there is no graduated income tax, some of them would be Ebenezer Scrooges and not help the poor in any way, either directly, by welfare, or indirectly (for example, by creating jobs for them).

The more moral a people is, the less government correction of the free market there needs to be. In a society of saints, there would be no need for such measures because private voluntary charity, motivated by a sense of justice and compassion, would take over, and the rich would voluntarily take care of the poor, not keeping them poor by calling them victims and demanding nothing from them, as a socialist government all too often does, but by giving them their needs in exchange for challenging them to work and help actively for both their own and the common good.

So the moral quality of individuals is the single most important cause of a good or a bad society.

What is the single most important cause of morally good or bad individuals? There is no question about the answer to that one. Massive and uniform social science gives us the answer: families. Stable, loving families. Children learn to make the fundamental choice in life, whether to be good persons, that is, just and charitable persons, or to be bad persons, that is, selfish persons, between the ages of five and twelve. And that choice is determined by three things: by themselves, of course, since they have free will; by their friends and social influences even more; and by their parents even more. Let's say it's 10 percent their free will, 20 percent friends and society, and 70 percent parents.

The four most happy, prosperous, peaceful, and stable societies in history all had two salient characteristics: they were very moralistic—we would call them "preachy"—and they had a very high view of the family. They are the Mosaic, the Confucian, the Islamic, and the Roman. They lasted 3500, 2100, 1400, and 700 years, respectively. They were far from perfect, but they were notably more successful and stable than any others in history.

These four societies were also founded on four religions: Judaism, Confucianism, Islam, and Roman polytheism. Religion has always been the strongest moral indicator in the world. This is simply an empirical fact. Those antireligious agitators who deny this fact are simply being dishonest. Everyone knows it's true, and so do they, but they cover it up, they lie about it. They probably lie to themselves first before they lie to you. Statistics prove it, but you don't need statistics. Everyone knows it. If you're walking alone down a dark street at night and you see a really big man approaching you and you see he has something in his hand but you don't know what it is, what happens to your fear of being harmed by him when you get close enough to notice that it's a Bible?

So family and religion are the two main causes of individuals being morally good; and morally good individuals are the main causes of a good society. So the two most crucial causes of the common good are morality and religion.

Quod erat demonstrandum.

13

Seventeen Freedoms

All freedom is negative freedom. Freedom is always freedom *from* something implied to be bad. But since freedom is itself only negative, the word does not tell us what replaces this bad thing. It can be good or bad, better or worse.

Thus there are fake freedoms, false freedoms, freedom from *good* things—for example, anarchy, which is freedom from rule, or lawlessness; and irresponsibility, which is freedom from responsibility.

There is physical freedom (which is the only kind, according to materialists like Hobbes), which is simply freedom to move. Meteors have this until they land, and balls until they're caught.

There is medical freedom, or health, which is freedom from disease. There is neurological freedom, which is comfort, or freedom from pain or physical suffering.

There is military freedom, which is peace, freedom from war, or victory, freedom from defeat.

There is personal economic freedom, which is freedom from poverty. There is also public economic freedom, which is free trade, a free-market economy.

There is emotional freedom, which is happiness or freedom from depression or emotional suffering.

There is psychological freedom, or free will, which is the freedom from determinism. This freedom is ineradicable, but it is diminishable by the inner determinisms of addictions. We are not all cocaine addicts, but we are all selfishness addicts or sin addicts, so our free will, though inviolable, is vulnerable.

There is religious freedom, or salvation, which is freedom from sin (that is, sanctity) and the guilt and punishment attendant on sin.

There is also political religious freedom, which is the freedom to practice your religion without government interference, illegality, fines, or persecution. This is under attack today in some significant form in every single country in the world except the Vatican.

There is intellectual freedom, or freedom from ignorance. This is called knowledge or wisdom.

There is moral freedom, which is sanctity, or freedom from vices. It is closely connected with religious freedom or salvation from sin, but "sin" is a "vertical", religious word, while "virtue and vice" do not explicitly refer to the vertical dimension, the relationship with God.

There is eschatological freedom, which is freedom from Hell, from eternal death.

There is ontological freedom, the freedom from destruction of your existence—in other words, immortality.

There is personal freedom, freedom from slavery, from being property instead of a person.

And there is political freedom, which is liberty or freedom from tyranny.

Use these distinctions as you will. But use them.

14

Four Confusions about Freedom

Our culture's attitude toward freedom is ironic and paradoxical. For we value it enormously, more than ever before in history; yet we feel, deep down, that we have less of it than before, less than our "founding fathers" had.

There is a parallel paradox about power. Through our spectacular technological successes, we have far more power over nature than ever before; yet we feel more and more impotent. We would be less able to survive a catastrophe like a nuclear winter than our ancestors. And among us, the least "advanced"—farmers, peasants, boy scouts, those who live today as we lived centuries ago—would survive most easily.

What explains the paradox? Let us consider a hypothesis, a thought-experiment. Let us suppose that freedom has become our addictive idol. All idols crash, and all addictions blind even as the idols to which we are addicted are crashing. Perhaps we are Gollum, and freedom is our One Ring. It is called "the Ring of Power", of course, not "the Ring of Freedom"; but freedom, after all, is almost identical with power. You are neither free nor powerful if you are poor, paralyzed, oppressed, enslaved, imprisoned, tyrannized, chained, ignorant, sick, in great pain, or dead. Everyone repeats Lord Acton about power corrupting; why does no one ever say that about freedom?

Might our confusion about freedom come from our addiction to it? Or might the causality work both ways?

In any case, we are confused about freedom. Since I am an intellectual prostitute, that is, a professional philosopher, a philosophy "professor", I will try to sort out the confusion.

We are confused in at least four different ways about freedom, confused about four different distinctions that have to do with freedom. I will list these distinctions in an order: from the one that is most concrete and therefore easy to see and to agree about to the one that is the most abstract and therefore harder to see and to agree about. They are:

1. the distinction between church and state as visible, public institutions and, thus, between religious freedom and political freedom;

2. the distinction between the private and the public sectors of life and, thus, between private and public freedom;

3. the distinction between persons and ideas or between personal subjects and mental objects; between thinkers, who are free, and thoughts, which are not; and

4. the distinction between three different kinds of freedom, namely:

a. positive freedom, freedom-for rather than freedom-from; teleological freedom—the freedom that Augustine called *libertas* (liberty)—which is the freedom from failure to attain our intrinsic, natural end, destiny, beatitude, happiness, flourishing, fulfillment, perfection, or greatest good (for Christians, Jews, and Muslims, this means freedom from sin);

b. free will or free choice—the freedom that Augustine called *liberum arbitrium*—which is freedom from determinism; and

c. political freedom, which is freedom from tyranny, oppression, and slavery, whether to the state or to private slave-owners.

I begin with the clearest and most institutionally concrete of my four distinctions: what we today call "the separation of church and state" as visible institutions.

The idea was not widely popular until the seventeenth century, when it became almost necessary for the survival of Western civilization, since the more we fought wars with religious passion, the more the wars became total wars. For nothing merely earthly or secular, not even survival, could trump the Will of God as an absolute.

The solution was put in place most notably in the Peace of Westphalia, which ended the Thirty Years' War, a war between Catholic and Protestant states that was the most traumatic and devastating war in our culture's history. In some parts of Germany, a third of the civilian population was slaughtered. The Peace of Westphalia instituted religious freedom of choice for principalities, and later this was extended to individuals.

Nearly everyone today agrees that the solution was a good one and that the politicization of religion was a bad thing. Looking at the consequences of our own past religious wars and at present Islamic wars against both non-Muslims and "heretical" Muslims, the vast majority today in the West agree that those wars are very bad for both religion and politics. Believers agree that the politicization of religion is bad for religion, and unbelievers agree that the religionizing of politics is bad for politics. So both parties agreed to a divorce, or at least a separation.

But a consequence of this agreement has been the confusion between two distinctions: the distinction between church and state and the distinction between the private and the public sectors. By confusing and conflating these two distinctions, "the separation of church and state" has become the

privatization of religion, the removal of religious voices from
what Fr. Neuhaus has called "the naked public square", to
such an extent that it is illegal to pray, but not to blaspheme,
in public schools, to display the Ten Commandments on
public land or buildings, or to offer religious grounds for
public policies about America's real religion, which is sexual
autonomy. It has become illegal "hate speech" to confess
in public that you believe at least one thing in the Bible, its
condemnation of sodomy. In England, those who believe
this cannot adopt children or even foster children. Thus,
not only some public *behavior* but also private *beliefs* (at least
about this cherished issue) are becoming illegal. In Canada,
it is now illegal to say there are only two genders or even to
use the words "mother" and "father" on public documents.
We are no longer moving toward *Brave New World*, we are
in it. This is not the separation of church and state, it is the
exact opposite: the institutionalization of a new church, or
anti-church.

This is not toleration of pluralism or of religious freedom;
it is the exact opposite: intolerance of pluralism and of religious freedom. The freedom of religion has been curtailed
by the demand for the freedom from religion. The two parts
of the First Amendment have been set against each other,
and the "no establishment" clause is suffocating the "free
exercise" clause.

This has happened because the distinction between church
and state has been confused with the distinction between
the private and the public sectors of society. This is clearly
fallacious. Religion cannot be identified with or limited to
the private sector, because religion calls for a public wit-
ness, both in words ("evangelization") and deeds ("social
justice").

This confusion between distinction #1 (between church and state) and distinction #2 (between private and public) is based on a third confusion, about a third distinction, which also concerns freedom. This is the abstract and philosophical but practically crucial distinction between persons and ideas.

People who call themselves "liberal" or "progressive" tend to treat ideas (at least all ideas outside of science, especially moral ideas about sex and religious ideas connected with them) as subjective and with skepticism. Subjectivism and skepticism are not the same, for subjectivism says that nobody can ever be known to be wrong and skepticism says that nobody can ever be known to be right. But both serve the same gods of "equality" and "nonjudgmentalism". Progressives are in fact very judgmental toward the "judgmentalism" of conservatives. "Don't you dare be dogmatic", they say, dogmatically.

This is obviously self-contradictory. "Do not judge ideas" is an idea. "Do not judge moral ideas" is a moral idea. "Do not make universal claims" is a universal claim. "There are no meta-narratives" is a meta-narrative. But some say that logic itself is only an invention of dead white European heterosexual religious males for the suppression of Democrats.

Traditional ("conservative") wisdom tells us to be tolerant of people, even stupid and wicked people, but intolerant of stupid ideas and wicked behaviors; to love sinners but hate sins. In fact, the whole reason for hating sins is loving sinners, as the whole reason for a surgeon to hate cancer is his love for his patient's health.

Christians' three highest authorities all command us to be "judgmental". St. Paul tells us to "test everything; hold fast what is good" (1 Thess 5:21). St. Peter commands us to "be prepared to make a defense . . . for the hope that is in you" (1 Pet 3:15). And if we are to make a defense for our hope, we must first have one; and to have one, we must find one; and to find one, we must seek one, critically and "judgmentally". Finally, Christ Himself tells us to be tough-minded as well as tender-hearted, to be "wise as serpents" as well as "innocent as doves" (Mt 10:16).

But what our current confusion has wrought is the exact reversal of this. "Test everything; hold fast what is good" has been changed to "Hold fast only to not holding fast to anything, but do not test that idea." "Make a defense for hope" has been changed to "Do not hope for anything from reason outside the sciences." And "Be wise as serpents and innocent as doves" has been changed to "Be wise as doves (just coo) and innocent as serpents" (hiss at that "basket of deplorables").

"Who am I to judge?" has been transferred from its proper object, persons, to its improper object, ideas and actions. So far, this has extended only to things desired by the Sexual Revolution. But it is inevitable that this moral relativism will spread from the sex organs to the other organs, since the organs of the soul, like those of the body, are related by an organic unity.

This third confusion, the one between three kinds of freedom, is really about the relation between freedom and truth. Modernity demands freedom *from* moral and religious truth rather than freedom for it. Truth has been made relative to freedom rather than freedom relative to truth. It is no longer the truth that will make you free; it is freedom that will make the truth. The means and the end, the relative and the absolute, the human and the divine, have exchanged places. Pope St. John Paul II diagnosed this disease long ago, in *Veritatis Splendor*, which is the second most hated papal teaching of our time, next to *Humanae Vitae*. In fact, it was hated

precisely because it supported the philosophical principle behind *Humanae Vitae*. For in order to relativize sexual morality, it is necessary to relativize moral truth in general. But
to do that, something positive must attract the wandering
planet away from its sun of truth. What better second sun
than freedom?

Freedom now trumps truth. That is why we have suddenly embraced not only the obvious insanity of calling the
murder of our own unborn children "choice" and sodomy
"marriage" but even the right of a man to be, and to be
treated as, a woman simply because he wants to. After all,
at the heart of liberty is the right of each man, not God, to
determine the meaning of life and the mystery of existence.

I distinguished three kinds of freedom: political freedom,
free will, and teleological freedom. Most people who are
not sociologists still believe in free will, and most people
believe in political freedom. But the freedom that is the most
important one of all is the one that has suffered the most
pervasive denial. This is the freedom to become what we
are designed to be and supposed to be. For "what we are
supposed to be" is no longer widely believed to be anything
more than what we ourselves suppose ourselves to be. To
the modern mind, it is not an objective reality. The finish
line is invented by the runners. No longer may we invoke
either nature or nature's God as the source of any natural
ends. To put it bluntly, we have internalized the motive of
the first sin of Satan, who would not serve, only command;
who insisted on the ultimate freedom, the freedom to play
God. The ancient Greeks named about five hundred gods,
the Romans five thousand, the Tibetan Buddhists nine million, but Americans are the most polytheistic people in history: they have named 330 million gods.

This is not one of the three kinds of real freedom distinguished above. It is a fourth freedom, a false freedom, the freedom to be God. That is the root of our insanity. We demand to be our own authorities because we demand to be the authors of our own being and meaning. But once we can play God, we can play any game at all: Aryan superiority, transhumanism, transgenderism, consumerism, sexism, spiritualism, materialism, pantheism—anything. Who knows what future fashions will offer? It can be whatever advertisement we fall for. And advertising, which is the world's oldest profession, was invented You Know Where by You Know Who back You Know When: "You shall be as gods."

How bad can it get? Read *Brave New World* to see. How long can it last? Fortunately, not long. Insanity is not favored by natural selection.

15

Is Agnosticism in Religion
the Default Position?

I had been asked to speak on the topic: "Is agnosticism or skepticism concerning religious questions the only reasonable and/or honorable position?"

I began by proposing two minor changes to the title: I think we should take out the two "ors". First, let's just say "agnosticism" instead of "agnosticism or skepticism" for three reasons, all of which strengthen the Yes answer to our question that I will try to refute. I don't want to shoot ducks in a barrel, after all.

First, "skepticism" is a conclusion, the conclusion of a debate about epistemology; it is a doctrine, the doctrine that certainty is impossible—while agnosticism is only a personal attitude, and only an initial and hopefully provisional one, thus easier to defend.

Second, skepticism has the problem of apparently being logically self-contradictory in all its forms: Is it true that there is no truth? Is it certain that there is no certainty? Is it an absolute that there are no absolutes? Is it objectively true that truth is not objective?

Third, "agnosticism" is usually associated only with religion, while the term "skepticism" is not so limited, and thus skepticism is harder to defend because it is more general.

I would also like to remove the second "or" and say "reasonable *and* honorable" instead of "reasonable *or* honorable", so that we can argue two questions rather than one: is agnosticism reasonable intellectually, and is it honorable morally? These are two good reasons for agnosticism, not just one. Again, I want to meet the strongest position, not the weakest.

Let me say right off the bat that I think agnosticism *seems* to be both reasonable and honorable, but upon more careful thinking, it is not. I will give reasons for both of these two opinions: first, for why it seems to be so and, second, for why it is not so, or my own position.

It seems to be the only reasonable and honorable position because it seems to follow from a premise with which nearly everyone will agree: that we ought to be open-minded and unprejudiced in our search for truth in any field, including religion.

And open-mindedness is both reasonable and honorable because it is both a hypothetical imperative and a categorical imperative; that is, it is both a practical or pragmatic or instrumental value as the most effective means to the end of finding the truth and also a moral value, a duty, because it follows from the "golden rule", since we always want others to practice open-mindedness both toward ourselves and toward objective reality.

This position also seems to have three very intelligent and serious thinkers to defend it: Socrates, Descartes, and Clifford. (The Oxford philosopher, not the big red dog.)

Socrates is nearly everyone's model of an ideal philosopher, and Socrates always followed the argument wherever it led. He sought not personal victory but truth. Though he had definite opinions, he always had strong logical reasons for them. He questioned every idea, and questioning is an expression of agnosticism, for we question what we do *not* know, and "agnosticism" means literally "not-knowing". As you all know, he was declared wise by the Delphic oracle because he alone knew that he was *not* wise. As Jesus divided people into sinners who thought they were saints and saints who thought they were sinners, Socrates divided people into fools, who thought they were wise, and the wise, who knew they were fools.

Second, in his *Discourse on Method*, the book that birthed modern philosophy, Descartes formulated a four-step method that seems ideal for honest systematic thinking about anything, and its first and most important rule is to practice universal methodic doubt. If we begin with doubt, we may end in certainty, but if we begin with certainty, we will probably end in doubt. *People* should be treated as innocent until proved guilty, but *ideas* should be treated as guilty, that is, false, until proven innocent, that is, true. This rule, more than anything else, has accounted for the fact that modern science has succeeded so much better than premodern science. If you want to think scientifically, the authority of Aristotle, of theologians who did not know science, or even of common sense should not settle any idea as either true or false. It must be tested by doubting and experimenting. In the empirical sciences, this means empirical experiments; in philosophy, it means thought experiments.

Finally, Clifford's Rule states that we should always proportion our beliefs in any idea to the evidence for that idea; that it is always morally as well as intellectually wrong to accept an idea upon insufficient evidence. Conclusive evidence for any idea is rational justification for believing it, while conclusive evidence against it justifies rejecting it; probable evidence for it justifies probable or provisional belief, while probable evidence against it justifies provisional rejection; and lack of evidence, or roughly equal evidence for and against the idea, justifies suspension of judgment, or agnosticism.

Take this principle as a major premise, add the minor premise that there is usually good evidence both for and against essential religious ideas such as the existence of God, the immortality of the soul, or the veracity of mystical experience, and it logically follows that we should be agnostic about such ideas.

That agnosticism is the default position, then, seems almost self-evident. Why do I doubt it?

First, of course, because Socrates, Descartes, and Clifford all tell me to doubt everything, and therefore I will doubt them, too. No question should be forbidden. To demand scientific proof for *every* idea even seems logically self-contradictory, since there is no scientific proof for *that* idea. The same is true if we speak of proof in general: there is no proof of the proposition that every proposition must be proved. It is only a practical postulate, and opposite postulates do not disprove each other as contradictory propositions do.

But there are more positive and specific reasons for being agnostic about agnosticism than merely this problem of formal logical self-reference.

Let's examine our three authorities more carefully. Socrates was the great enemy of the Sophists, but it was the Sophists who were the agnostics, as well as skeptics, while Socrates was quite *certain* of at least a few very important things, and most of those things were religious. The three most important of them were: first, the veracity and trustability of the Delphic Oracle and of his own "daimon", his "inner divine voice", both of which he never doubted, even though they told him very strange and apparently irrational things; second, the certainty, stated twice in the *Apology*, that "no evil could ever happen to a good man whether in this life or in the next", since the true self is the soul and its evils, which are folly and vice, come from within, not from without; and third, that the cause of evil is always ignorance: ignorance of yourself, ignorance of the fact that what you always want, happiness, comes only through virtue, which is the care for the soul, which is the true self. Socrates was agnostic about the name and the nature of God but not about His existence. Nor was he agnostic about the ultimate good or goal of human life, or about everyone's duty to be virtuous. In fact, an agnostic like Edith Hamilton was so upset by the Socrates of the *Gorgias* that she used her worst possible insult: she called him "an evangelist".

As for Descartes, he himself says in the *Discourse on Method* that his method of doubt is only for science and philosophy, not for life or religion, and to be practiced only by the few, not by the many. To use the scientific method on your spouse or on God would be not only inappropriate but insulting, and its result would not be the discovery of new truths but a just rebuff.

Finally, Clifford's Rule is in the same boat as Descartes': it is unlivable outside the laboratory or the library. No friendship could be formed, much less a marriage, if we were not prejudiced in favor of our friend or our spouse. So Clifford's Rule implicitly assumes that religion is more like science than like marriage or friendship; that it deals with abstract ideas, not persons; that God is not a Person but a Principle; and thus it implicitly presupposes the falsity of the claim of religion, that God offers Himself in friendship or spiritual marriage, the proper response to which is personal trust rather than scientific curiosity. That assumption has a name; it is called atheism. That is hardly an unprejudiced assumption.

When approaching any subject with an open mind, for example, when reading a book written by someone else, the first essential is to listen, to open your mind to the thoughts of the other before you judge. So we need to listen to religion before judging it. We need to let a religious book like the Bible or the Koran speak to us before we speak to it. It is always wrong to interpret a book by your own beliefs or principles; you must try to interpret it by the author's!

I here simply assume that Deconstructionism is disastrously wrong when it says that this is impossible. In fact, though I will debate with anyone, even a Nazi, or a fanatical New York Yankees fan, I will not debate with a Deconstructionist, because the first and most minimal requirement for honest debate, the belief in and desire to know objective truth, is deliberately excluded by the very essence of Deconstructionism.

Scholars tend to be the worst offenders against this rule of listening. Most books about poetry are written by writers with no ear for poetry. Most philosophers who write about humor are appallingly humorless. They lack the inside view, the listening ear. The same is often true of religion.

I will listen to an atheist who has listened to the thing he disbelieves. If, for instance, someone like Freud tells me that he thinks Christianity is a form of insanity, the world's greatest collective hallucination, or the world's greatest piece of wishful thinking fairy tale, and then explains it by a powerful human motive like fear, I will listen with interest and respect. If I read someone like Samuel Beckett with a deep sense of black metaphysical humor at the irony of waiting for a no-come, no-go Godot, I will laugh with him, or perhaps at him, but I will laugh delightedly. If I read someone like Camus agonizing over the dilemma that the meaning of life is to be a saint, but you can't be a saint without God and there is no God, I will listen with deep sympathy. If I read an Ivan Karamazov's anger at the permissiveness with which God runs this awful world, I will deeply admire him.

But if someone tells me that religion is simply a system of platitudes and moralisms, I will not cast my pearls before swine; I will be deaf to him because he has been deaf to the thing he is pontificating about. He has not listened. If this thing is not true, it is the biggest, cleverest, most deceptive lie ever, and the vast majority of all the human beings who have ever lived have been, quite frankly, insane, for God is no more than Jimmy Stewart's "Harvey", a thirteen-foot-high invisible rabbit that an otherwise sane adult takes as central to his life.

We all agree, I hope, that honesty is a moral absolute. (If you do not agree, please accompany the deconstruction-ist and the "platitudes and moralisms" atheist back to the pigsty while the rest of us argue in the jeweler's shop about whether the pearls we are examining are fake or authentic.)

Honesty is a *motive*. So we should explore what motives lie behind agnosticism and what motives lie behind religious belief, both when first embraced, by religious conversion, and when maintained in the face of doubts and questions later on.

I do not suggest a single answer to this question. I only suggest that it be seriously asked. The question can only be answered by each individual, of course. So I address you alone, the individual. No one else is in this room right now, only we two. Are you truly open-minded? Do you want to be totally open-minded? Or do you want to win a debate and appear more clever than your opponent? Are you willing to look seriously at the evidence contrary to your position? Have you invested much time and effort in listening to your opponent, whether this is the religious believer or the un-believer? How many such people do you know, personally? How often have you talked about religion with them?

Religion must be either the most important truth in the world, if it is true, or the most important illusion in the world, if it is false, for it has been at the center of more people's lives than anything else in history. Not to care about whether it is true or false is certainly not to be honest and open-minded.

Thus, the believer should read the great atheists: Voltaire and Nietzsche and Sartre and Russell and Camus and Beckett. And the unbeliever should read the great theists: Augustine and Aquinas and Pascal and Dostoyevsky and Kierkegaard and C. S. Lewis—and let's not forget Jesus.

The believer should pray: "God, if you are not what I think you are, please do not let me persist in my illusion, because I want above all to know the truth. I don't want to believe in Santa Claus even though that belief made me more happy and more moral every Christmas. I am tough-minded. I can take it." And he should pray that often.

And the unbeliever should pray: "God, if you are really there, please correct me and convince me, because I want above all to know the truth. If you are real and you love me, don't let me miss you." And he should pray that often. Because an agnostic, by definition, though an unbeliever, is not an atheist any more than he is a theist; an agnostic does not know that God is *not* there any more than he knows that God *is* there. If there is even a chance of God being there, and you don't pray that agnostic's prayer, if you do not perform the relevant experiment, if you do not seek, then either you are not an agnostic but an atheist, or else you are not honest and open-minded but terrified of finding God and wanting very much not to find Him. Or else you have no self-esteem or reasonable care about yourself and your life. For if you inherit a deed for a multi-million-dollar mansion and you do not even take the trouble to examine the deed to find out whether it is authentic or a fake, then you obviously do not even care about living a richer life.

For just consider what is promised by religion. It is not

merely an eternal mansion with an eternal fire-insurance policy. It is infinite, incomprehensible, unimaginable ecstasy, spiritual orgasm, something of which the deepest earthly joys are mere shadows or appetizers, something that satisfies your heart's deepest hunger for joy and your mind's deepest hunger for understanding. It is the Face and Mind of the Maker, the Author of the play in which you are now acting, the play that is called Human Life.

Pascal says there are only three kinds of people: those who seek God and have found Him, those who seek Him but have not found Him, and those who neither seek nor find Him. The first, he says, are reasonable and happy: reasonable because they have sought and happy because they have found. The second are reasonable but unhappy: reasonable because they seek and unhappy because they have not found. The third are not only unhappy but also unreasonable, because they will not seek. There is no fourth class, who find without seeking.

The most fundamental dividing line, for Pascal, is not between the believers and the unbelievers, between those who have found God and those who have not. The most fundamental dividing line is between the seekers and the non-seekers, because that is the dividing line between the honest and the dishonest, the open minded and the closed minded, those who care about truth and those who do not. And Pascal implies that is also the dividing line between Heaven and Hell. For Pascal's supreme authority, whom he believed to be God Himself in the flesh, promised that all who seek will eventually find, implying that those who do not seek will not find, ever. And obviously Jesus was talking about seeking and finding God, not anything else.

In conclusion, I do not wholly disagree with the position that agnosticism should be the default position.

It is the right default position for some, at the beginning, at least: for those who have never believed or been taught religion.

But it is not a good default beginning position for those who *have* been taught and who have once believed and who still have some good reasons for believing. For them, *belief* is the default position, just as marriage is the default position for one who is married, even if unhappily and uncertainly; and friendship is the default position for friends, even if they are quarrelling. For persons, unlike ideas, should be treated as innocent until proved guilty.

Agnosticism can be a good default position only temporarily, not forever, for there is no forever in this life. There is only finite time. We are, as Pascal says, "embarked", and our ship's fuel is finite. Refusing to put in at either the home port of theism or that of atheism for lack of certainty, for lack of guarantees, is guaranteed and certain to end in failure. Agnosticism can only be temporary. Waiting until certain evidence is in before you say either Yes or No in religion, as distinct from science, is like waiting until Romeo proves to you that you should elope with him and telling him every day neither Yes nor No but Wait. You will wait forever, for lovers do not propose by laboratory experiments or syllogisms.

Lovers say two things: I Love You, and I Promise You Can Trust Me. Those are precisely the two things the God of the three Abrahamic religions says to us.

But perhaps there is no God, no Romeo, no marriage proposal, no promise. There is evidence both for and against God. That is the fundamental justification for agnosticism in the first place.

Ah, but if the evidence is ambiguous enough to justify agnosticism instead of atheism, why not make the theistic wager? Why not say Yes to Romeo? What can you lose? Truth, of course, but agnosticism says you can't prove the truth either way. Remember, we are not refuting atheism, only agnosticism. What else can you lose? There is only one other thing all of us want absolutely: joy. Your only chance of winning that is to wager Yes, and your only chance of losing it is to wager No. Pascal is right: if you want the joy you never got on this earth, if your heart is big enough to desire more than painlessness, political correctness, and pornography, there is only one chance of getting it: if there is a God. And you can't be *sure* there isn't. Romeo whispers in your ear; are you too much of a coward to say Yes to him, even though you can't see him? What can you lose? Almost nothing. And what can you gain? More than everything.

And *after* you make this wager and *live* it, you will see more and more clearly that it was the right wager—very much like marrying the right person. And if it was not the right person, if you are abused, you are always free to divorce. But you can't do that unless you first take the marriage vows, which is what agnostics refuse to do.

Dostoyevsky speaks of his religious faith as emerging "from the furnace of doubt". Faith like his is unshakable because it has already been shaken. Honest religious faith, as distinct from mere personal convenience, does not come from avoidance of the hard questions but precisely from confrontation with them and from the hope that, whether the other things Jesus said are true or false, at least this one thing is true: "Seek, and you will find."

16

A Word about Islam, and a Defense
of My Controversial Book about It

Between Allah and Jesus (IVP, 2009) may well be the most controversial book I have ever written. Two opposite classes of
people will be very suspicious of it for the same reason: it
treats Islam too positively.

First, secularists and "liberal" or "progressive" Christians. They fear Islam because it is not only a religion but
a very, very *religious* religion. All the things they see wrong
with religion, they see exacerbated in Islam: that it is absolutistic, fanatical, exclusivistic, triumphalistic, chauvinistic
and militaristic. In other words, it's too "conservative".

But I think many conservative Christians, both Catholics
and Protestants, will also dislike my book because it seems
too "liberal", too optimistic, too naïve. After all, Muhammad was a false prophet, and Islam is a heresy that spread
by force and fear. Islam is to religion what Nazism is to politics. That is the thesis of many Christian writers on Islam
today (for example, Robert Spencer). What are they miss-
ing? How can I justify my more positive "take" on Islam?

I am tempted to feel justified by this double reaction by
comparing it with the similar double reaction to Jesus, from
both the theological Right and Left of His day. But such an
analogy, like all analogies, *proves* nothing (though it may *suggest* something). I am also tempted to justify my attitude by
comparing it with that of John Paul II and Benedict XVI.

But instead of arguing from authority, I want to explain and justify the main point of my book, which is that Christians should learn something about their own religion from Muslims, something very important and something nearly all Christians seem to have forgotten. I could call it its *power*, or perhaps its "primitivism".

When we use the word "primitive", we almost always confuse two things: (1) "early in history and, therefore, simple" and (2) "stupid, clumsy, and embarrassingly bad". The first meaning does *not* logically entail the second.

There is a law of history that applies to nearly everything; yet this law is seldom understood. It says that *all "progress" concerns means, not ends*. Thus progress always comes in the technological sophistication of anything, but not in its core, its essence, which is by far the most important.

Take movies. All movie lovers know that modern movies are so far advanced in technological "bells and whistles" that they make old movies look embarrassingly "hokey". But movie lovers also know that only one out of a hundred modern movies has characters or themes that are not shallow compared with the old classics. There are great exceptions (*The Godfather*), but they are just that: exceptions.

Take art. Modern art is "sophisticated", even when it cultivates "primitivism". But primitive art has a power we simply cannot re-invent, because art comes from the soul, and the modern soul is shallow as a frying pan.

Take philosophy. There is a power in Socrates, Plato, and Aristotle that has never been equaled, despite the fact that we now have far more adequate techniques of logical analysis.

Take religion. Each religion's scriptures have produced trillions of words of commentary, yet they have an unrivalled "primitive" power.

Take technology itself. Agriculture, the domestication of animals, and the control of fire are far more important to civilization than nuclear bombs, space travel, or computers. And they have an unparalleled power to fascinate a five-year-old, and the five-year-old who still lurks in the heart of all of us. The affection of a dog or the fascination of fire never ceases to amaze us, but moon rockets do, after a while.

Take language. Primitive languages like Hebrew are like giants, and modern languages, though far more complex and sophisticated, struggle in vain to communicate the *power* in words as primitive languages can.

Take economics. The basic, common-sense lessons of work and reward, time management, and supply and demand are far more important, more certain, and more effective than all the different controversial contemporary systems.

Take the *results* of successful economics in life. A "primitive" is poor but appreciative and happy. A sophisticated modern is rich but spoiled and bored. Africa is the poorest continent in the world, yet Africans smile more than anyone else. Louisiana is one of the poorest states in America, but the happiest. (This is the result of recent sophisticated scientific studies.)

Take ethics. "Be good", "Do unto others", and "Love people" are more effective, more motivating, and more conscience-compelling than any more sophisticated theory or system.

In all these fields, we can say, with Robert Fulghum, "Everything I really need to know I learned in kindergarten." Everything else is mere means, mere mechanism.

We can expect the same in religion.

Islam has many problems today. But it is the world's simplest religion, the world's most primitive religion, and that is not one of its problems. Its essence is the bare, simple essence or core of all authentic religion: total surrender, total submission, total conformity to the Will of God. It is the essential formula for sainthood, which is the ultimate *end* of religion. God designed the whole universe as a saint-making machine, after all. And if we forget that end for one moment, distracted by the gears and wheels—if we forget the end in our concern for superior means—we fall flat on our sophisticated faces.

Yes, Islam is "primitive". Chesterton says: "The fear of the Lord, that is the beginning of wisdom, and therefore belongs to the beginnings, and is felt in the first cold hours before the dawn of civilisation; the power that comes out of the wilderness and rides on the whirlwind and breaks the gods of stone; the power before which the eastern nations are prostrate like a pavement; the power before which the primitive prophets run naked and shouting, at once proclaiming and escaping from their god; the fear that is rightly rooted in the beginnings of every religion, true or false: the fear of the Lord, that is the beginning of wisdom; but not the end" (*St. Thomas Aquinas, the Dumb Ox*).

That fear of the Lord is the foundation of our religion, though it is not the capstone. It is the beginning, though not the end. But if we try to erect a building on another foundation, it will fall. The most beautiful thing about a plant is its fruit or flower, not its root. But the plant will not grow from any other beginning; it will not grow backward. Without justice, no real charity. Without the fear of God, no real love of God.

Europe is a spectacular example of a sophisticated, cultured, sensitive, advanced, compassionate continent that is dying because it has repudiated its "primitive" roots. It will soon be a Muslim continent—necessarily so, because it is uprooted while Islam is rooted, and only rooted plants grow.

If we want to grow the Christian field, if we want to expand Christ's kingdom, we must recapture those roots, that fear, that absolute abandonment and awe-struck adoration, that "Jesus-shock" (to quote another book title). We can re-learn it from our separated Abrahamic brothers: from Orthodox Jews and from pious Muslims.

17

Pity vs. Pacifism

I was reading *The Lord of the Rings* for the seventh time when I was struck by an apparent contradiction. It was the apparent contradiction between Tolkien's approval of pity and his disapproval of pacifism. Actually, what I was struck by was the fact that I, like nearly everyone else, thought of this as a contradiction, while Tolkien did not.

Tolkien is certainly not a pacifist. The battle scenes in the book, and even more in the movie, are magnificent, not only in the telling (in both the book's words and the movie's images), but also in the doing. Even the most ardent pacifist must have a slumbering admiration for the heroic "good guys" charging the Hellish "bad guys" in scenes like the battle of the Pelennor Fields in the siege of Gondor:

> We heard of the horns in the hills ringing,
> the swords shining in the South-kingdom. . . .
>
> Arise, arise, riders of Théoden!
> Fell deeds awake: fire and slaughter!
> spear shall be shaken, shield be splintered,
> a sword-day, and red day, ere the sun rises!
> Ride now, ride now! Ride to Gondor! . . .
>
> Out of doubt, out of dark, to the day's rising
> I came singing in the sun, sword unsheathing.
> To hope's end I rode and to heart's breaking:
> Now for wrath, now for ruin and a red nightfall!

In every human heart there lies the conviction both that war is terrible and that heroism is wonderful. And that heroism is clearest in the war poets, like Stephen Spender:

I think continually of those who were truly great,
Who, from the womb, remembered the soul's history
Through corridors of light, where the hours are suns,
Endless and singing . . .
Born of the sun, they travelled a short while toward the
     sun
And left the vivid air signed with their honor.

Yet it was the same deep mind and heart, that of Tolkien, who at the heart of his plot exalted pity, or mercy, as the only thing that could save Middle-earth. Tolkien was no wimp. He clearly had both Elves and Ents in his ancestry, and his son Christopher, in his draft induction form, filled in the blank labeled "father's occupation" with the word "wizard". Yet this great man's greatest heroes were not wizards or warriors but hobbits: Bilbo, Frodo, and Sam, all of whom saved Middle-earth by *pity*, by mercifully sparing Gollum when they could have justly killed him when reason and prudence seemed to counsel that. For it was Gollum alone who completed the task at the Crack of Doom that neither Frodo nor anyone else could have done. Thus Gandalf said, sagely and prophetically, "the pity of Bilbo may rule the fate of many."

When I first noticed this contrast, I simply ascribed it to Tolkien's voluminous heart and his open-minded love of paradoxes (apparent contradictions), especially the traditional paradox of justice and mercy, or the "just war", on the one hand, and pity and mercy, on the other hand. And I remembered that that was the very paradox at the heart of our salvation, at *our* Crack of Doom, on Calvary, where

Christ fulfilled both divine justice and divine mercy, with the same stroke.

But then another thought came to me: these two things are not only reconcilable, not only not a real contradiction; they are not even a paradox, an apparent contradiction! The value and heroism of a just war, on the one hand, and that of pity or mercy, on the other hand, naturally go together in the same philosophy of life, the same "world and life view". And most people do not see that. They divide the options into the one or the other. They see pacifism as the natural complement of pity and a just war as the alternative to both. In other words, they put the two P words together, "pity" and "pacifism". But Tolkien did not. He saw them as opposites.

I asked myself why, what was behind this; and I came up with the following "big picture".

There are four possible world views. The best one, the Christian one that was Tolkien's, exalts pity but not pacifism. It is typified by Locke and Lincoln in our world and by Faramir in *The Lord of the Rings*, the character Peter Jackson got the most completely wrong in his movie. It is the philosophy of the noble knight, the gentleman, both gentle and manly:

> War must be, while we defend our lives against a destroyer who would devour all; but I do not love the bright sword for its sharpness, nor the arrow for its swiftness, nor the warrior for his glory. I love only that which they defend: the city of the Men of Numenor; and I would have her loved for her memory, her ancientry, her beauty, and her present wisdom. Not feared, save as men may fear the dignity of a man, old and wise.

The second world view is that of paganism, which both Machiavelli and Nietzsche tried to restore in our world and which is typified by Boromir in *The Lord of the Rings*. It admires neither pacifism nor pity. It is the code of the warrior.

The third world view is that of the majority of people in Western civilization today. It is the philosophy of Rousseau and pop psychology, which admires both pacifism and pity and which sees them as natural allies. It is out of pity that it embraces pacifism.

Pity is seen here as a feeling or sentiment rather than a mercy, since the concept of mercy is meaningless except against the background and assumption of justice and, thus of a universal and objective natural moral law, which Rousseau and our civilization have rejected.

The fourth world view is the one we are moving toward in our postmodern "brave new world" of "soft totalitarianism" (De Tocqueville's prophetic term), in which pacifism is no longer an option but an orthodoxy that is enforced without pity or mercy. But this is a new kind of pacifism: it is not military but spiritual. The very idea of spiritual warfare, of real evil as well as real good, must logically disappear with the disappearance of the natural law, so the only remaining evil is the *idea* of evil, the idea that there might really be such a thing as an evil, an enemy, and a just war and, thus, the possible need for pity and mercy. Mercy presupposes and goes beyond justice; postmodernism has not yet got that far.

I am haunted by the startling prophetic statement about this fourth world view made by Fr. Richard John Neuhaus that "when orthodoxy becomes optional, it will soon become forbidden." The very existence of the Christian conscience, which authorizes both heroism and mercy, is an intolerable burden to the "soft totalitarian". It is a light that exposes sin. And if there is sin but no salvation, if there is justice but not mercy, if pity becomes, not mercy and forgiveness, but mere soft sentiment, then that typical misunderstanding of Christianity becomes intolerable. Nietzsche showed that with striking clarity when he confessed that he could not live in a world with a God who saw his dark side, his own inner dwarf. Nietzsche hated pity above all other things and literally began to go insane when he felt pity for a horse he saw being abused in the street. Sartre, too, felt the same terror at "the eye", the eye of the God who saw everything, including his own soul, which "under the eye" was no longer free to lie to itself about itself, to be its own dark God.

Everyone who has ever been imprisoned and tortured by a tyrant knows that the tyrant is not satisfied to be lord of others' bodies. He must, like Satan, be lord of their souls and their minds. The very existence of their free minds threatens him because those minds reflect the light of truth and justice. The tyrant can have no pity on the notion of pity or mercy, because mercy means going beyond justice, and that assumes justice and, therefore, natural law and, therefore, real evil and, therefore, spiritual warfare. The tyrant requires spiritual pacifism.

Our civilization has moved through three world views: from paganism (no pity and no pacifism) to Christianity (pity but not pacifism) to modernity (pity and pacifism). It is now moving to postmodernity, which is a new pacifism, a pacifism without spiritual warfare, a war on the very notion of spiritual warfare, and a war without pity or mercy for its enemy.

It is time to turn back the clock two turns, from postmodernity to modernity and from modernity to Christianity. As Chesterton says, "You can't turn back the clock" is a simple lie. You can. And you must, if it is keeping bad

time. Even three turns of our historical clock, back to ancient paganism, is better than none, because paganism at
least believed in a real justice and, therefore, could be con-
verted to adding mercy and pity. Paganism was like a virgin,
and Christianity like a wife, and modernity like a divorcee.
We've not gone back to paganism; divorcees are no longer
virgins.

So what, then, is the image for postmodernity? I'd suggest
a B-movie title: "the curse of the spider woman".

18

Judgment

There are at least nineteen different kinds of judgment that we should distinguish. I'm sorry I could not find a twentieth, to match the number of digits on our fingers and toes. But nineteen does match the digits of Frodo Baggins, one of my heroes. (I'm sure you remember Frodo of the Nine Fingers and Gollum of the Eleven.)

The importance of the topic—judgment—is obvious. For one thing, making judgments is a privilege of persons only. For another thing, it is necessary, both to live well on earth and to enter Heaven.

I will say one thing about each of these nineteen kinds of judgments. It may not be the most important or most fundamental thing about them, but it will be a point I believe is important enough to take a few minutes of time to think about.

The first kind of judgment is judgment as such, judgment in the abstract. I mean the logical form of judgments: the affirmation or denial that a predicate belongs to a subject, that some state of affairs is true or is not true. This is "the second act of the mind" in traditional Scholastic logic and the only one that contains truth.

The first act of the mind, simple apprehension or conception, does not contain truth because it merely conceives concepts, which are neither true nor false, but are the raw material or contents of true or false judgments. Thus, neither the concept "apples" nor the concept "fruits" is true or false, but the judgment "apples are fruits" is true.

And the third act of the mind, reasoning, moves from the presupposed truth of one or more judgments, as premises, to the truth of another judgment, as the conclusion to be proved.

Concepts tell us *what*, judgments *whether*, and reasoning *why*. We understand essences in concepts, existence in judgments, and causes in reasoning.

Because concepts attain only essences while existence is attained only in judgments, this essential logical structure of thought implies the distinction between essence and existence, one of the most important principles of metaphysics and the basis for Aquinas' best proof for the existence of God, the proof from contingent beings to a necessary being —that is, from the premise of the existence of beings whose essence is *not* existence to the conclusion of the existence of a being whose essence *is* existence as the only adequate answer to the question of why these other existing things exist. If their existence does not come from within their own essence, it must come from outside, from a cause. Only a Being whose essence is existence can explain the existence of beings whose essence is not existence, as their cause. Only a Being that explains itself can explain the beings that do not explain themselves.

The distinction between essence and existence and between concepts and judgments also explains why St. Anselm's famous "ontological argument" is invalid: it confuses essence and existence, treating existence as an essence or "what" or property. If you didn't follow that, you'll just have to take my word for it now. My point here is how centrally important it is that only judgments attain ontological existence and logical truth.

When we investigate concrete particular judgments rather than the universal abstract logical form of judgments, (my second point), we find that they are made either by humans, by angels, or by God, who are the only three kinds of personal beings we know.

Let's look at human judgments first, for obvious reasons.

Within human judgments, the most fundamental distinction is between theoretical and practical judgments, that is, judgments of truth and judgments of goodness. All judgments are made by the intellect, but theoretical judgments regulate thought while practical judgments regulate practice, life, or action. So our second kind of judgment is the theoretical judgment.

It is very significant, and the primary cause of the decline in the popularity of classical education, that the words "theoretical", "speculative", and "contemplative", have all lost their honorable connotations in our culture. Instead of referring to truth, the words "theoretical" and "speculative" both now connote "uncertainty". And "contemplative" is limited to monks and mystics.

This is a symptom of deep cultural decay and stems largely from Francis Bacon, who announced a radically new *summum bonum*, or greatest good, for our culture: the conquest of nature by applied science. In other words, not truth, but power; not conforming the human mind to reality, but conforming reality to the human will.

An icon of this cultural decadence can be seen near my hometown, in Cambridge, Massachusetts. It is supremely ironic that "Veritas", "Truth", the official motto of the flagship educational institution of America, Harvard University, is a word that is never uttered inside that campus in most of the humanities courses there without ironic quotation marks around it.

In a Baconian civilization, our art forms, especially movies, tell limitless lies about life but infallibly improve their special effects. In other words, technology trumps truth.

Enough about the second kind of judgment, theoretical judgments of truth. My next eleven kinds of judgment will all be practical judgments about goodness. And the first one of the eleven—judgment number three—is a judgment about practical judgments, namely, the judgment on the part of most modern philosophers that there is an absolute gap between theoretical judgments of fact and practical judgments of value.

This dogma of the absolute fact-value distinction is the justification for moral relativism, the idea that values are relative to our subjective feelings and choices rather than to objective truth. Moral relativism is the disease that C. S. Lewis, a sophisticated and polite Oxonian, said "will certainly damn our souls and end our species".

It will damn our souls because salvation requires repentance, which in turn requires admission of sin, which in turn requires a real, objective moral law to sin against, which means objective values. It will end our species because it amounts to a consciencectomy, as in *Brave New World*. Those people are not humans; they are yuppies. Their bodies look like persons, but their souls look like puppies.

If values and facts are not absolutely distinct, if values are a special kind of facts, then moral values can be objectively real and there can be a natural moral law. (Notice how much more uncomfortable and demanding the word "law" is than the word "values".) But if not, not. If the fundamental principle of morality is that "Good *is* to be done and evil *is* to be avoided", then *ought* depends on *is*, ethics depends on metaphysics and on reason. If, instead, morality is simply the command of the will that makes the rules of the game, then moral law is a dictate of will, not of reason—which is the philosophy of Nominalists, Asharites, fundamentalists, Euthyphro, Ockham, Machiavelli, Hobbes, Rousseau, Marx, Hitler, and Satan. God says "Come let us reason together." Satan does not. God appeals to reason, Caesar appeals to force.

Unless our Caesars are classically educated, in the tradition of Plato and Aristotle. On the very first page of Plato's *Republic*, there is a little scene that sets the fateful choice for Western civilization. Socrates, with a few companions, meets a larger group of friends, and there is a contest of wills. The larger group wants Socrates to change his plans and come with them, and their spokesman says to Socrates, "You see how many we are, so either dig in your heels and stay here or else fight us." And Socrates replies, "Surely there is a third alternative: that we *persuade* you that you *ought* to let us go." Rational moral persuasion—the key to the good society for Socrates, Plato, Aristotle, and medieval Christendom. And we? Are we Platonists or Machiavellians?

If we believe in a real natural moral law, a fourth kind of judgment becomes possible: the judgment about these real moral goods.

The word "good" has three basic meanings, says Aristotle, the master of common sense: the moral good, the pleasant good, and the useful good. Judgments about pleasure and utility can still be made without a natural moral law, but real moral judgments cannot.

Aquinas sees these judgments as most fundamentally about *ends*. Like Aristotle, he is teleological. Kant sees them as most fundamentally about *duties*. But both believe reason can make moral judgments because reason knows the moral absolute, whether it is the ultimate rational *end* of Eudaimonia—blessedness, true happiness—or the ultimate rational *duty* of the Categorical Imperative. It is not feeling or

desire or passion that makes moral judgments, but reason
—reason in the old, honorable, broad, ancient sense rather
than in the narrowed modern computerlike sense. Philosophers who deny that moral judgments are made by reason,
philosophers like Hobbes, Rousseau, Hume, Mill, Marx,
and Russell, do not have an incomplete moral philosophy;
they have none at all, just as a primitive who makes up fan-
tastic stories about the constellations does not have a primitive astronomical science but has no science at all.

A fifth kind of judgment concerns how we can rightly
make these moral judgments. How can we judge *how* to
judge morally? And the answer comes from our two paragons
of common sense, Aristotle and Christ. Aristotle says we
must *be* good in order to make good moral judgments; that
we must cultivate moral habits, and, thus, moral character,
by repeated right choices of the will if we are to be morally
wise and perceive moral good and evil rightly with the intellect. The will should obey the intellect, but the intellect
also needs to be educated by the moral will. The good will
tames the intellect as a woman tames a man. It's like the
classic line from the movie *My Big Fat Greek Wedding*: "The
man is the head of the household, but the woman is the
neck that turns the head."

Christ appeals to this same psychological principle in
speaking of the religious good when he answers the Pharisees' question "How can we understand your teaching and
whether it is from God?" by saying that "If your will were
to do the will of God, you would understand my teaching
and that it is from Him." That is the basic principle of biblical hermeneutics in one sentence.

A sixth kind of judgment is the prudential judgment
about how to attain pleasure, happiness, or joy—three ever-
deepening levels of the same thing, though we do not have
a single generic word for it—the thing that is desirable for

its own sake rather than as a means to some further end, but not because it is our moral duty, but just because it satisfies our restless heart. Some fools judge pleasure to be enough, and some misjudge even what things will give them pleasure (money, power, and drugs are obvious examples). But pleasure and even happiness get boring; only joy satisfies us. So if we are wise, we will not compromise this goal or settle for anything less. In other words, we will give Aquinas' answer to God's question to him, "You have written well of me, Thomas; what will you have as a reward?" Thomas' answer was: "Only Yourself, Lord." Have three wiser words ever been spoken?

A seventh kind of practical judgment is judgment of utility: What means will best attain our end, whether the end is pleasure or morality? Experience is the only answer to how to judge what to do to attain pleasure; but the Commandments, both externally revealed to Moses and internally known by conscience, are the answer to how to judge what to do and what not to do to attain moral goodness. These Commandments are very easy to know and hard to obey, so our sophists have cleverly solved that problem by making them harder to know and easier to obey, or at least harder to disobey—in fact, making them harder to disobey precisely by making them harder to know, that is, by nuancing them and juggling them and doing fancy little dances around them. The first sophist was the Devil, in Eden: "Did God really say *that*?"

An eighth kind of judgment is not the judgment of natural law or natural good but positive law and positive goods, that is, man-posited, man-made laws, human laws. This is the kind of judgment made by professional lawmakers, professional law-enforcers, and professional law-interpreters, that is, congressmen, policemen, and judges. I have little to say about judging what laws to make or how to enforce them better, but I have something to say about judging what the motive for sanctions and punishments must be, because it is an answer most intellectuals in our society now deny. The essential motive for punishment should *not* be rehabilitation or deterrence, but justice. Even though charity is the highest motive, and your personal motive for rehabilitation is charity to the criminal whom you want to rehabilitate, and even though your personal motive for deterrence is also charity—to possible future victims that you want to protect —while the personal motive for justice, even when it is not confused with vengeance and hatred, is not this personal charity—yet it is essential that justice be the first motive and the absolute standard. Otherwise, we will give unjust, undeserved punishments just because we think they will work better to rehabilitate or deter. Judgments as to what will rehabilitate or deter are uncertain because they depend on our very fallible predictions of the future and our very fallible understanding of the criminal's character. Judgments of positive-law justice, on the other hand, do not depend on these two uncertainties and, thus, can be much clearer. And so are judgments about natural-law justice, to everyone but a sophist.

A ninth and closely related kind of judgment that is often made by federal judges or supreme court judges in our society today in interpreting the law is often called "dynamic", "creative", "progressive", or "flexible" interpretations. These are what allow "judicial activism". It is exactly parallel to "dynamic", "creative", "progressive", or "flexible" interpretations of the Bible, by which you can make the Bible to teach pretty much anything you want, from flat earth science to Communist revolution. The same judicial philosophy that, in *Dred Scott v. Sandford*, found that Blacks were only semi-human and property rather than persons, found the privacy rights in the Constitution's "penumbra" that justified the murder of a baby in the womb. It might find anything else there tomorrow—anything at all.

The philosophical principle of such judicial activism is simple: we do not discover and obey truth, we create it with our judgments. Truth is the subordination of thought, not to reality, but to our will. In the words of Justice Anthony Kennedy in *Casey v. Planned Parenthood*, "at the heart of liberty is the right to define for oneself the meaning of life and the mystery of existence." In other words, "God, you have to get out; you're sitting in my seat."

Still another kind of positive judgment—this is our tenth kind—is made, not by individual judges, but by a public community as a whole. This used to mean representational democracy, in which important issues were decided by the judgment of concrete individual persons, by popular vote, either directly, by referendum, or indirectly, by electing representatives. Today, it is the unelected media and the *Zeitgeist*, the "spirit of the times", or climate of opinion they create that determines the most important issues. It is what De Tocqueville prophetically called "soft totalitarianism". The most influential philosopher who defended this is Rousseau, with his notion of the infallibility of "the general will". It is "the general will", or the *Zeitgeist*, that influences the judgments of our unelected judiciary on such momentous issues as redefining marriage. The issues judged by the judiciary are typically much more culturally, morally, and personally important than the largely economic issues determined by Congress or the President.

Another way of classifying judgments is in terms of their personal objects. We can judge God, ourselves, and others. Let these be our eleventh, twelfth, and thirteenth kinds of judgments.

Regarding judging God, I have already mentioned one

way this is now done, by a "creative" interpretation of the law. A creator, as distinct from an interpreter, has no data and no bounds, so that his judgments are never wrong. Moose are large and geckos are small only because the real world limits our creativity, but elves can be either large, as in Tolkien, or small, as in Shakespeare, whatever we desire. How do we do this to God? As the well-known quip goes: "They say God created us in his own image, but we've been returning the compliment to Him ever since."

Careful, though. Because there are many gods on the market, we *must* judge among the various candidates and, in that sense, judge God. Otherwise, we simply arbitrarily decree which god is God. And the two standards are truth and goodness, rationality and morality. We *must* judge any logically self-contradictory god and any evil god to be false and unworthy of belief, because we have these two absolute standards in our own souls that are absolute, indubitable, and self-justifying. We literally cannot believe anything that is so irrational as to be self-contradictory, and therefore literally meaningless, even if we call it God; and we literally *cannot* accept what is intrinsically unacceptable because it is logically self-contradictory to love what is known to be really, literally unlovable intrinsically. God Himself has placed these two prophets in our conscience, and when we use them honestly and in submission to objective truth and goodness rather than our own will, we judge with divine authority. A meaningless self-contradiction does not suddenly become meaningful and believable, and an intrinsic evil does not suddenly become good, when someone says "God can do it." God can do what is physically impossible but not what is logically or morally impossible. That is why Christ had to die: because God could not simply pretend we had not sinned or say "Justice? Forget about it."

Our twelfth kind of judgment is judging ourselves. This is subject to a cruel trilemma. If we judge ourselves, we must find ourselves either morally good, morally wicked, or halfway in between. If we judge ourselves as morally good, we become self-satisfied prigs and Pharisees. If we judge ourselves as morally wicked, we become self-loathing worms who cannot love our neighbors as we love ourselves because we cannot love ourselves. And if we judge ourselves as halfway between, as mediocre, as wishy-washy, we are luke-warm Laodiceans who deserve the shocking divine word of judgment in Revelation 3:16. The word is: "vomit". Look it up.

The solution is simple: we should judge our sins but not our selves. If we habitually look at God instead of ourselves, we will not succumb to any one of the three horns of the trilemma, for in the light of His face, we cannot judge ourselves to be worthy, worthless, or waffling. None of the saints ever thought any one of those three things.

Our thirteenth kind of judgment, judging other individuals, is, as we all know, dangerous and forbidden by Christ Himself because judging persons as distinct from actions is God's prerogative. Of course, that does not forbid us to judge actions, for to do that would undermine all morality.

Today there is only one class of people who always deny this distinction, between sins and sinners, actions and persons; who say that their whole personal identity is what they do and, therefore, if we reject what they do, we reject what they are; that to hate their life-style is to hate them, the whole, the person, the I. That is a religious judgment, to identify something with the whole self. These people who support this new religion now rule the media, in fact, so well that I would probably be prosecuted for "hate speech" if I dared to identify them, though we all know who they are. They are the only people in the world, other than Muslim terrorists, who are obeying Churchill's formula for winning a war, whether a military war or a culture war: "Never, never, never, never, never give up." Their latest victory is transgenderism. It will not be their last.

All thirteen kinds of judgment so far are made by humans. There is a fourteenth kind of judgment because there exists, in addition to humans, one other known species of created persons, namely, angels. Their judgment, according to "The Angelic Doctor", Thomas Aquinas, is more like that of a woman than that of a man: intuitive rather than ratiocinative, "big picture" synthetic rather than step-by-step analytic. Therefore, they are good instruments of divine providence, being closer to the mind of the Author of our human drama than we are. We should cultivate their friendship and pray for their inspirations and trust them when they come, because their judgments are by nature wiser than ours. (This is also true of women, by the way, if I may speak as a man to other men and pretend that women are not listening and giving us that "I told you so" look that makes us feel and look like deflated tires.)

Finally, God judges in at least five ways: to create, to identify, to provide, to incarnate, and to consummate. He gives us our universe, our personal identity, our lifelong provision, our salvation, and our glorification.

He created the universe freely, not necessarily, so He judged that it was good to create, both before and after He created. That is judgment number fourteen. "Good, good, good", He muttered, judgmentally, after each day's work of creation. The answer to the atheist's strongest argument, the problem of evil, is here, in this judgment: that it was better to create a large family of mankind even foreseeing that they would be severely retarded delinquents, than not to create us at all, or even not to create anything at all, and to keep everything safe and perfect, like a yuppie couple who refuse children. Thank God, God is a little crazy.

But we cannot rationally justify God's judgment that it was better to create than not to create, for there is no higher standard, no premise, from which we can deduce that conclusion. If the universe were necessary, we could be sure of it; but since it is contingent, we can only be thankful for it.

That is judgment number fifteen, and divine judgment number one. Judgment number sixteen, and divine judgment number two, is the judgment that it was not only good but "very good" to create us in His image. Since God's own eternal essence, revealed only once, to Moses in the Burning Bush, is Person as well as Being, I as well as AM, He shared that image, that I-ness, that personhood, that subjectivity, that spiritual self-consciousness, with us. And since He is the Author of our very existence, we have no identity apart from Him any more than Hamlet has identity apart from Shakespeare. When He said "Let there be Peter Kreeft". He judged this confused, fearful ball of animal string that rolls down the world's gravity slopes unraveling the strands of its identity with every turn to be something good to create. And even though that is crazy, it is sacrilege for me to disagree with Him, to judge contrary to His judgment.

Our judgment number sixteen, and divine judgment number three, is divine providence. The three presuppositions of divine providence are the three most nonnegotiable premises of theism, that God is all-powerful, all-wise, and all-benevolent. To judge all three as true logically entails the astonishing conclusion of Romans 8:28, that He works all things, even evils, together for our ultimate good if only we let Him by trusting Him and loving Him and entering into the bloodstream or life-stream of His will, which directs all the growth of our souls and bodies by what He judges best for us in the end.

It is certainly difficult to believe this and to trust Him that much, as Job discovered in his own experience, but it is as necessary as it is difficult. For the alternative is to deny either His omnipotence, His omniscience, His omnibenevolence, or the laws of logic—all of which are nonnegotiable. He is our perfect guru, and every event He brings into our life is a move on His chessboard against the Devil and the Devil's pawns, which are the world and the flesh—and God does not make any wrong moves or lose any games. His judgment is perfect.

Judgment number seventeen, and divine judgment number four, is His judgment that it was best to incarnate His Son to give His body and blood—all twelve pints of it—for our salvation. This, too, is a judgment we cannot understand or prove by any prior premises that are available to the human mind and, therefore, one that we can only accept with gratitude and wonder, as we accept creation and providence.

Gabriel Marcel made famous the distinction between problems and mysteries: problems can be solved because they are outside us; mysteries cannot because the solver is himself the problem. In Marcel's words, "A mystery is a problem that encroaches upon its own data." God judged the problem of human life to be a mystery and solved it by *becoming* it. "He made him to be sin who knew no sin, so that in him we might become the righteousness of God."

Judgment number eighteen, and divine judgment number five, is "the last judgment". To consummate our creation, providential preservation, identity, and redemption, God gives us our perfection, our sanctification, and glorification. If we saw, in our present condition, the perfected

saint that we are destined to be in Heaven, we would probably fall down on our faces in idolatrous worship. It is His
mercy that keeps us in ignorance of our own future glory.
But He gives us hints. In the Song of Songs, the divine
bridegroom says to His human bride, "You are all fair, my
love; there is no flaw in you." That is the last judgment.
What is usually called the Last Judgment is preliminary to
that: the separation of the sheep and the goats, the saved and
the damned, the ones who say to God, "Thy will be done"
and the ones to whom God says, "Thy will be done" (to
quote Lewis again). All get what they want: the damned get
justice and the saved get mercy. The next-to-last judgment
is justice, but the last judgment is mercy.

Since this is written for you, the reader, number nineteen
is *your* judgment on it now, on all eighteen points of my
judgments about judgment. I can only say to you what I
will say to God at the Last Judgment: I am not such a fool
as to ask for justice, only for mercy.